The Way We Build

THE WORKING CLASS
IN AMERICAN HISTORY

Editorial Advisors
James R. Barrett, Thavolia Glymph,
Julie Greene, William P. Jones, and
Nelson Lichtenstein

*A list of books in the series appears
at the end of this book.*

The Way We Build

Restoring Dignity to Construction Work

MARK ERLICH

UNIVERSITY OF ILLINOIS PRESS
Urbana, Chicago, and Springfield

All photos by Ellen Webber.

Library of Congress Cataloging-in-Publication Data
Names: Erlich, Mark, 1949– author.
Title: The way we build : restoring dignity to
  construction work / Mark Erlich.
Description: Urbana : University of Illinois Press, 2023.
  | Series: The working class in American history |
  Includes bibliographical references and index.
Identifiers: LCCN 2022055979 (print) | LCCN
  2022055980 (ebook) | ISBN 9780252045196
  (cloth) | ISBN 9780252087332 (paperback) | ISBN
  9780252054570 (ebook)
Subjects: LCSH: Construction industry—United
  States. | Labor unions—United States. | Building
  trades—United States.
Classification: LCC HD9715.U52 E75 2023 (print) |
  LCC HD9715.U52 (ebook) | DDC 338.4/762400973—
  dc23/eng/20230210
LC record available at https://lccn.loc.gov/2022055979
LC ebook record available at https://lccn.loc.gov/2022055980

To Graham, Iza, and Rose
and the futures they will build

Contents

Acknowledgments

I have been part of the construction industry for half a century. I worked as a carpenter in the field for the first part of my career and then was elected to serve in various union leadership positions for over twenty-five years. During that time, I was exposed to an incredible assortment of people who make that crucial sector of our economy work. Tradesworkers, contractors, developers, political leaders, and community activists are just a few of the components that sometimes work in harmony and sometimes in conflict, but always make a fascinating stew. I received an education that could never have been replicated in a classroom and I am enormously grateful to everyone whose path I crossed.

I have also tried to be a useful writer and have relied on a variety of colleagues for feedback on my projects. This book is no exception. My initial thought had been to take up the widespread "future of work" commentary and question prevailing assumptions as they applied to construction work. I subsequently determined that in order to have a helpful analysis of the future, it would make sense to re-visit the past and explore the present, all from the perspective of the impact on those who work in the industry. As a result, this book has its own past, present and future. Successive drafts have taken substantially different forms.

Throughout the process, I sought comments and criticisms from both old and newer friends. The book you are reading has benefited greatly from suggestions from Dale Belman, Sharon Block, Matt Capece, Jeff Grabelsky, Steve Herzenberg, Maurice Isserman, Mike Kazin, Tom Kochan, Claire Kovach, Joe McCartin, Russ Ormiston, Al Peciaro, Kris Rondeau, and David Weil.

Every one of them read a draft and responded. I appreciate the ideas they contributed. The book is far better for their recommendations and counsel.

The photos were taken by Ellen Webber, a gifted photographer and former colleague. I'm pleased that this book offers readers an opportunity to appreciate her work. A broader sample can be found at ellenwebber.net. Ellen took these photos when she was employed by the New England Carpenters Labor Management Program (since renamed the North Atlantic States Carpenters Labor Management Program). We are grateful for their permission and quick action to use the photos in this book.

Finally, I would like to thank Alison Syring Bassford, Acquisitions Editor for the University of Illinois Press. A friend referred me to Alison and I am very glad he did. She provided constant encouragement in the early stages when I was still struggling to articulate the overall concept and shepherded me through all the steps of the drafting and production process. The other people I've worked with at the Press have been similarly helpful. Writing a book is both an individual and a team venture, much like a construction project.

The Way We Build

Walking a beam.

A Tale of Two Cities

"To build a house is a fine trade in
youth; in age it must be a religion."
—Mark Turpin, *Hammer: Poems*[1]

I joined the Carpenters Union in 1975 after working for a few years as a non-union carpenter/woodworker, and became, in turn, an apprentice, journeyman, foreman, and superintendent. I left the jobsite in 1988 to serve as the field director for the campaign to defeat a ballot referendum aimed at repealing the Massachusetts prevailing wage law. I subsequently went to work at the Massachusetts Building Trades Council until 1991. The following year, I ran for office against an incumbent and was elected business manager of my Boston-area Local 40. When the Carpenters Union was restructured into regional councils in 1997, I served as organizing director and then, again, defeated an incumbent for the position of executive secretary-treasurer (ES-T) of the New England Regional Council of Carpenters in 2005. As ES-T, I headed up a 24,000-member organization covering six states and supervised 100 people on staff. I also chaired our union's training, health, and pension funds until I retired in 2017. Those years provided an incredible education, opportunity for trial and error, and exposure to members, leaders, and activists in and outside of my union who hoped to revitalize the building trades and the labor movement. This book is an attempt to reflect on my experiences, draw on what I learned, analyze what I saw, summarize historical developments, and offer suggestions of best practices for union revival in construction.

I was fortunate to work in a union city. At the time, union conditions were common in most American cities. I knew enough about the history of the industry to recognize that, for decades, the building trades had offered generations of workers an opportunity to earn a decent living. My predecessors were once referred to as "labor aristocrats," sometimes sarcastically, often critically, but almost always with a sense of wonder and envy. They rode the wave of the post WWII Great Compression, the last period in U.S. history that witnessed a general decline in income inequality as the average rate of worker pay outpaced income growth to the wealthy. Construction workers did even better. Their inflation-adjusted hourly earnings surpassed most occupational groups, climbing from $14.59 in 1947 to $36.09 in 1971, a nearly two-and-a-half-fold increase.[2] The vast majority of trades workers could not access higher education, yet their skills offered them an alternative pathway to the American Dream and allowed them to experience a sense of pride and dignity unavailable to most blue-collar workers or, apparently, professionals. A 1954 survey about the meaning of work for five different occupational groups concluded that skilled craftsmen had a higher degree of self-respect, self-expression, and sense of purposeful activity than steelworkers, coal miners, salespeople, and physicians.[3]

Unlike even the most skilled factory workers who were tied to tasks performed at one station, construction workers exercised a degree of autonomy in their duties, moving from job to job and different locations within a site. In 1981, an upstate New York construction executive observed of his colleagues that "the journeyman is trained to perform organizational and planning functions that in other industries are the responsibilities of management." He continued, "I marveled, that men, left alone to work and plan independently, can produce with intelligence and skill such creative results."[4]

The workforce was dominated by generations of Irish, Italian, and other men of European ancestry. It was a white male world. Census figures from 1940 show that only three percent of non-white employment was listed in the craftsmen category, and fewer than one percent of employed women worked in construction.[5] Particular ethnic groups were often associated with certain trades and occupations. Some unions even established foreign-language speaking locals to accommodate first-generation immigrants. For the most part, it was a community-based, father-son, uncle-nephew handing down of skills, opportunities, and access. As a young plumber reported in 1958: "My whole family are plumbers and I just followed along."[6]

Hub Dillard, a forty-eight-year-old crane operator, described construction work in Studs Terkel's classic *Working* as "eating dust and dirt for eight, ten hours a day." But Dillard went on to tell his interviewer that doing the job well was "food for your soul that you know you did it good. Where somebody walks by this building you can say, 'Well I did that.'"[7] Dillard's comments have been echoed by successive waves of trades workers who proudly show family and friends the projects they worked on in their communities. The contrast between the challenging jobsite environment and the spirit of craft pride animated tradesmen through most of the twentieth century. Angelo Bruno, a Western Massachusetts carpenter, fondly recalled his union's regular dinner dances: "We knew we weren't all a bunch of tramps because we all got dressed up. We didn't always go around with mud in our shoes and dirt on our clothes."[8]

Construction has always been and continues to be dusty, dirty, difficult, demanding, and dangerous work. The industry can still serve as a conduit into a middle-class lifestyle. Kelvyn Carasquillo recently joined a union apprenticeship program while living in a homeless shelter with his wife and child. "It's been life-changing," he said. "I'd been seeing my buddies go into selling drugs. But I like this work. I feel productive. I like to wake up and feel like I'm part of building my city." Similarly, Jenaya Nelson referred to her entrance into the trades as a "life changer." She heard about a union program in a welfare office when she was a twenty-one-year-old single mother. "I'm feeling very secure now," referring to her journeyworker status. "Thanks to the union, I was able to get my own house after six months."[9]

Construction may be the most visible of all major industries. Laborers dig utility trenches on city streets; carpenters set forms for the foundation walls of suburban tract developments; ironworkers connect high steel while tower crane operators maneuver materials on the upper floors of skyscrapers. The public nature of the industry allows bystanders to view the collaborative effort that contributes to the creation and repair of homes, buildings, roads, and bridges. Busy onlookers will slow their brisk pace, transformed into sidewalk superintendents peering through a chain link fence or portholes in a plywood barrier to watch as projects come to life with the hands and tools of an army of trades workers. Most people operate out of sight behind office doors, storefronts, and factory walls, but construction workers can be seen every day in every community practicing their crafts. For all the visible nature of the work, however, the terms and conditions under which trades workers toil are largely unknown and invisible.

The prospect of routine and comprehensive upward mobility has not been the only narrative in construction's last half century. While Carasquillo's and Nelson's stories represent both a continuation of the opportunities the industry provided in the past as well as serving as examples of the expanded race and gender diversity of newer entrants, the rungs on those ladders have been gradually worn thin by the emergence of a sizable non-union sector. Some non-union shops approximate union compensation, but many are characterized by reduced pay, few if any benefits, and hazardous conditions. Through the first seventy years of the twentieth century, the nation's buildings and highways were largely union built—private and public projects, non-residential and even many residential developments. Union hegemony provided the foundation for the beneficial contracts that had elevated wages. Real wage growth for union construction workers began in 1890 and continued for eighty years with little interruption despite two world wars and the Great Depression.[10] An alternate direction was charted beginning in the 1970s. Since 1971, average real wages for construction trades workers have plummeted by an astonishing 15%,[11] a function of the decline in union density and the corresponding growth of the lower-waged, non-union sector.

A survey conducted in 1936 reported that fully two-thirds of the nation's construction workers were union members.[12] In the post-war era, union density increased even further. By 1983, however, only 28% of wage and salary workers in construction were union members, and in 2020 that number had dropped to 13.4%.[13] Data from Leo Troy's 1985 *U.S. Union Source Book* tells a similar story. In 1947, construction union density was a remarkable 87.1%. By the time of the book's publication less than forty years later, it had tumbled to 23.5%.[14] Today, construction is a segmented, almost bifurcated, industry, no longer following a single ascending trajectory. In the remaining union strongholds in urban centers of the Northeast, Midwest, and West Coast, trades workers are paid well, receive extensive health and retirement benefits, and work in a monitored safety setting. They work on publicly funded prevailing wage jobs and large privately financed projects and frequently wield political influence at the municipal and state levels. However, most trades workers below the Mason-Dixon line, in the Southwest, Rocky Mountain states, and in suburban and rural communities across the country, generally work in an environment of lower pay, unsafe conditions, no benefits, no collective voice, and periodic wage theft. In 2019, the average wage of union construction workers was 47% higher than their non-union counterparts,[15] and the extent of that spread would be even greater if the value of union benefits were included and contrasted to the low compensation for those non-union workers in the underground economy whose very existence may not be captured by Census data. A recent study confirms that union construction workers' wages and access to health insurance and pension plans are comparable to those individuals with college diplomas, whereas non-union construction workers' compensation is on a par with high school graduates.[16] Another report found that today's construction workers are three times more likely than other workers to lack health insurance, and 39% of their families are enrolled in one or more public safety net programs.[17] The conditions many non-union workers face would have been unthinkable fifty years ago.

There is no need to romanticize the union world of work in the past to appreciate the security it offered. Racial and gender discrimination were pervasive and persistent. Layoffs were reminders of the work's precarious nature. Searing heat and frigid cold made jobsites unbearable. Physical demands were dangerous and exhausting. The tedium of repetitive unchallenging tasks could make the workday drag intolerably. Nepotism could trump merit in job assignments. Still, a union card in the pocket had been synonymous with a sense of craft pride and, while legacy tradesmen often took their protections for granted, membership guaranteed safeguards from the wage theft and unsafe conditions that are now standard elements of much of the non-union sector.

Frank Gomez started out in the 1990s hanging drywall on residential projects in the Gainesville, Florida, area, working from 7 a.m. to 5 p.m. every day with a single break for lunch, six days a week. He was paid on a piecework basis without any overtime, standing on inadequate planks twelve feet in the air. "Those planks are bending and you worry, but you worry more about how you're going to pay your next bill." Now a union organizer, Gomez looks back on his early days and shakes his head: "It was brutal."[18] Julio Beldi spent over ten years working as a non-union carpenter across New England. His pay ranged from $17 to $22 an hour, either in the form of a check with no deductions or in straight cash. Beldi received $18 an hour on a Veterans' Hospital in Rhode Island despite a law requiring a $50.69 hourly wage on the federally funded project, got no overtime pay for routine workdays of ten and twelve hours, no benefits, and frequently was not paid at all for weeks and even months as his company owners promised back wages only after they had been reimbursed by the general contractors. Collective bargaining agreements prevent these kinds of abuses from occurring. Now a member, Beldi concludes: "The union, for me, is the best."[19]

* * *

In late January 2020, I visited New Orleans with friends. I had heard that on October 12, 2019, an $85 million Hard Rock Hotel under construction downtown unexpectedly imploded, demolishing the partially erected eighteen-story structure, killing three workers and injuring dozens of others. In the months following the collapse, the local news media had tracked the appalling story of inaction as the developer, contractor, city officials, engineers, insurance adjusters, and attorneys engaged in an extensive finger-pointing exercise to assess legal and financial liability. The remnants of the building lingered unchanged and untouched, appearing to have been shelled by incoming artillery. Two of the dead bodies remained buried in the wreckage as authorities explained that removal might jeopardize the structural integrity of adjacent buildings. Shortly before I arrived, heavy winds had broken the ropes on the tarp that had been covering one of the deceased men nearly three months after the disaster. After his body became visible to pedestrians, the tarps were put back in place but no attempts were made at retrieval. At the time, I drove and walked along heavily trafficked Canal and Rampart Streets, looking at the building in disbelief at the utter disregard for human life. The remains of José Ponce Arreola, 63, and Quinnyon Wimberly, 36, were left in place, only finally recovered from the building ruins in August 2020. Arreola's and Wimberly's bodies had been invisible, then visible, and then ignored for over ten months.[20]

Both men were part of the large group of undocumented immigrants that have become a key presence on construction sites. A 2016 study estimated that undocumented immigrants make up 15% of the national construction workforce as the industry employs the largest share of undocumented workers in any major sector.[21] They work under the radar, frequently laboring for low wages and under substandard conditions, and can face reprisals and threats of deportation when seeking improvements. Workers had been regularly raising concerns about the shoddy architectural design, structural engineering, and project management on the Hard Rock Hotel. Days before the collapse, one of the tradesmen used his smartphone to document the lack of support for a newly poured concrete floor. Ordinarily, a forest of post-shore metal columns is placed from the floor below to support the deck while the concrete above is curing. His video showed an alarming lack of supports and at least one post-shore jack that was bent like a banana. The phone's owner's Spanish-speaking voice can be heard saying, "huge spaces without beams—look!"[22]

Delmer Palma was one of the survivors of the debacle. He narrowly escaped as the building's upper floors tumbled to the ground. During the months he worked there, he later claimed to have reported hazardous situations to supervisors on five separate occasions, only to be told to continue working. Two days after the collapse, Fish and Wildlife agents followed and questioned the Honduran native while he was angling in the Bayou Sauvage Wildlife Refuge. The agents immediately notified the U.S. Border Patrol and Palma was arrested. When Palma called his wife to let her know about his detention, she reported hearing one of the officers say in the background: "This is the [expletive] guy that is a survivor of the [expletive] Hard Rock building collapse."

Palma's attorney filed a complaint with the U.S. Department of Labor, suggesting that his client had been targeted and that his "employer instigated the immigration enforcement action." Lawyers representing other workers on the site indicated that the arrest had effectively eliminated further criticisms of the dangers on the job. "We've had a couple of guys who said specifically they don't want to take any action," noted attorney Darryl Gray, "because they fear having the same repercussions as Mr. Palma." When Palma's wife tried to contact some of his coworkers to encourage them to cooperate with a pending OSHA investigation, she was met with hesitation and fear. The federal intervention had a chilling effect. "They're not feeling safe," she said.[23]

Construction is notoriously unsafe, regularly ranking highest of any industry in total numbers of fatal work injuries.[24] Construction deaths account for 21% of all worker deaths nationwide,[25] and non-fatal falls are a recurring reality on job sites. After many years of decline, the fatality rate in construction has actually been increasing since 2011, a rise that may be partly attributable to the expanded reality of high-risk conditions, such as those at the Hard Rock Hotel project. Trades workers have always been concerned about safety, but the sense of feeling unsafe that Mrs. Palma described expands the parameters of dangers inherent in the job, dangers that now include risks of deportation and exploitation.

I would like to think that the Hard Rock story is a one-off, that it would never happen again. I would like to think that the tools and resources available in the twenty-first century would offer a solution for the safe and speedy removal of two dead construction workers from a building's rubble in a major American city. I would like to think that local political and industry leaders would never value a building's structural integrity over human dignity. Unfortunately, the brutal disregard for the fate of Arreola and Wimberly may be at the far end, but still on the spectrum of the treatment of some workers in a major industry. When Mrs. Palma said, "they're not feeling safe," she could have been describing the diminished sense of opportunity and security for a considerable segment of those who make a living in the trades.

Columns supporting a concrete deck.

Working on a window opening.

2

Snapshot of an Industry

The contemporary construction site would look familiar to someone who walked on a job at any time over much of the last century. Many of the innovations and inventions that remain common practices today were developed in the aftermath of World War II. The post-war interstate highway system, the increased demand for housing, and the extended economic boom prompted new materials, machines, and methods. The use of steel columns and beams and reinforced concrete had already successfully divorced the structural frame from the building envelope. The erection of partitions and ceilings had been separated from load-bearing structures, allowing architects and engineers to imagine bigger, taller, and more complex skyscrapers. With fewer structural restrictions, designers adopted open-plan interior spaces. Brick and other masonry, now given way to concrete and steel as the primary support material, was instead used as an ornamental application on the skin of a building. Clean water supply, efficient waste disposal, heating and air conditioning, effective power and lighting systems, safety and plate glass, and elevators in high rises had become standard components of the built environment.

Before the turn of the twentieth century, excavation had been conducted by horsepower and scoop and foundation trenches were dug by pick and shovel. By the 1950s, gas-powered heavy equipment machinery had substituted for most manual labor. John Deere introduced the first light machines intended for construction use in 1957, including front-end loaders and backhoes, all but eliminating back-breaking digging practices even on single-family homes.[1] Trucks carried pre-mixed concrete to the site, ending long days of hand-mixing, and new cement finishing machines smoothed large slabs.

High steel connections were welded. Gas and then electrically driven circular saws and drills replaced hand tools. Pipes were configured by power cutting, bending, and threading machines. The most commonly used materials were transformed. Plumbers shifted from lead to copper pipes while electricians abandoned metal conduit in favor of lighter and more flexible BX and Romex. Plywood and metal studs augmented wood planks and two by fours. Drywall superseded lath and plaster on interior partitions. Rollers and spray machines limited the utility of paintbrushes.

The current industry structure and dynamics also emerged over the last eighty years. In 2020, construction was a $960 billion business, representing over 4% of the nation's total Gross Domestic Product[2] and engaging over 11 million workers.[3] It has always been a highly volatile and unstable industry with annual seasonal swings and extreme boom and bust multiyear cycles. Since most construction projects are financed with borrowed money, the industry is highly sensitive to financial trends, credit availability, and fluctuating interest rates. Academics, journalists, and other observers often use construction as a barometer for general economic activity, as it typically enters recessionary periods ahead of most other industries. Furthermore, the impact on the national economy transcends the work performed on the job site since the supply chain that feeds those projects creates additional employment for multiple occupations. Almost a century ago, a Bureau of Labor Statistics study estimated that every hour of on-site construction activity produced two and a half hours of employment just in the producing, fabricating, and handling of building materials, let alone all the coffee shops and other establishments that support the daily activities of construction workers.[4]

Seasonality is a regular feature of construction. Cold weather regions often shut down road and bridge work during the winter, and building sites may be limited to interior tasks or portions of the project that can be heated. Provisions for snow, rain, and other natural disruptions are built into schedules as inevitable hurdles to completion. Yet it is the severity of the repeating business cycles that can drive trades workers out of the industry into lower-paying but more reliable forms of employment. The availability of work reflects the ups and downs of the broader economy. Construction unemployment rates are typically double that of the general population. Workers routinely lose the security of a weekly paycheck as they search for new jobs after projects are completed or miss work due to inclement weather. Economic recessions are regularly experienced as full-blown depressions in construction. During the Great Recession of 2007–2009, for example, construction unemployment topped out at 27.1% in February 2010,[5] months after economists declared the recession had officially ended—a figure higher than the peak of general unemployment in 1933 during the Great Depression. The oscillations of the past twenty-five years illustrate the vagaries of a reliance on construction as a secure source of work. In 1997, construction output in the U.S. (as measured by value added) was $340 billion and represented just under 4% of GDP. In the following decade, output more than doubled to $716 billion in 2007 and exceeded 5% of GDP in 2006, in part driven by the highly leveraged housing market boom. Then the bottom fell out. Output declined by a full 27% from 2007 to 2011 and construction's portion of GDP fell to 3.4%, indicating the disproportionate blow compared to other industries. Finally, a long and relatively smooth upswing followed, as output grew by 82% and construction returned to a more normal 4.2% of GDP in 2021.[6]

Within all of these broad gyrations, it is important to note that the construction industry does not generate one standard type of product. There are subsectors that have their own internal swings and misses. Residential and nonresidential as well as public and private spending all are affected by the inevitable business cycles to different degrees. The nonresidential category includes commercial, institutional, industrial, utility, heavy and highway, and other types of projects that do not rely on dwellings as their base component. Residential work can range from single-family homes to high-rise, multiunit apartment buildings. Overall spending on nonresidential projects is generally greater than on residential units, but in the red-hot homebuilding environment of 2006, the value of residences put in place actually exceeded nonresidential projects. The relative collapse was that much more acute as residential spending plummeted 59% between 2006 and 2011. Similarly, private construction spending that depends on credit tends to be more sensitive to the prevailing economic winds than public works. For example, federal, state, and municipal public spending on construction declined by a relatively modest 7% during the Great Recession. As a result, those expenditures played a useful counter-cyclical role in cushioning the shock, representing 22% of total spending in the industry in 2006 and climbing to 36% in 2011.[7]

The industry's products are fixed, durable, difficult to transport, and, as a result, inherently local in nature. The workforce usually lives within driving distance of the sites where they work and their employers remain mostly local and regional in scope. Ease of entry to employer status is unusually pain free. Access to a limited amount of equipment, basic power tools, a pickup truck, craft knowledge, business cards, a line of credit, and a measure of audacity are often the only ingredients necessary to open a small contracting business. The top fifty U.S. contractors may each earn over $2 billion in annual revenues,[8] but of the 745,207 construction establishments listed in the 2019 census, 90% operated with fewer than twenty employees, and over 65% with less than five. Less than three percent retained over 100 employees.[9] In 1949, only half of one percent of the nation's 400,000 residential builders erected more than fifty units a year.[10] In the interim, nonresidential and residential firms have grown larger, including numerous global giants, but nearly 70% of all construction firms still conduct their business from home.[11] And even those general contractors with sizable revenues often only employ management and office personnel, superintendents and a limited number of trades workers, relying instead on the vast array of small and medium-sized subcontractors that specialize in a single or a few trades and, despite their size, employ the majority of the overall field workforce.

There is no central stabilizing force comparable to monopsonistic sectors in which a few large companies establish uniform ground rules for buying and selling products and labor. On the contrary, construction's clashing, overlapping, competing, and occasionally feuding participants—owners, architects, engineers, bankers, brokers, contractors, and trades workers—produce an environment that was described by skyscraper builder William Starrett nearly a hundred years ago as "absolute anarchy." Starrett mused: "Is it any wonder that we have never met seriously to stabilize labor relationships?"[12] The multiple actors in construction, the decentralized nature of contracting firms, the high levels of worker skills required, the discreet character of local markets, and limited project duration combined to create a unique set of managerial challenges.

On the labor side, the difficulty of replacing skilled craftsmen and their organizational cohesiveness provided an unusual degree of leverage against a disorganized universe of employers. The Bricklayers Union was founded in 1865, and most of the other trades had union locals scattered around the country by the turn of the twentieth century. Starrett may have lamented the lack of organization among construction employers but, in reality, by the early 1900s, unions were the glue that held together an industry without a clearly defined management center. The owner/developer of a project may have hired the general contractors who, in turn, employed trades workers directly as well as engaged specialty subcontractors with their own workforce, but the unions' hiring halls supplied the labor force for general contractors and subcontractors alike. Starrett's comments underestimated the critical role of construction unions in injecting a high degree of order into the chaos. Since their inception, building trades unions have overseen the entry of new workers into the industry and referred workers on an as-needed basis to contractors working in their geographical jurisdiction, eventually providing basic training to apprentices, coordinating the members' health and retirement security benefits programs, and formalizing dispute resolution mechanisms to handle the inevitable day-to-day conflicts that arise in a fast-moving business.[13]

For the most part, contracting employers tolerated and even welcomed the unions' thorough intervention in labor relations. Union administration freed contractors to focus on business development, estimating, project management, and bill collecting—sufficient challenges for companies with limited office staff and relatively little experience with the nuances of labor relations. Loyalty to the union was not limited to the members. Many of the smaller subcontractors were often former union members who perceived their success as inextricably linked to the smooth functioning of the unions' programs. The remnants of the master journeyman-apprentice system of the guilds dating back to the Middle Ages had not completely disappeared. The twentieth-century version consisted of an alternate hierarchy of general contractor—subcontractor—journeyman—apprentice. In both scenarios, however, a cultural affinity of a shared work experience created bonds lacking in other major industries.

The small and medium-sized employers that dominated the industry had limited capacity to manage employment issues. They focused on the sufficiently complex tasks of bidding work and the subsequent execution of construction operations. Given the formal and informal connections between employer (particularly at the subcontractor level) and worker, most contractors were prepared to cede regulation of the labor market to the building trades unions in the United States, allowing them to function as the equivalent of the human resource departments for an entire industry. The rapid rise of union density in construction in the early part of the twentieth century was less a matter of successful missionary worker organizing than a grudging recognition that the unions offered solutions to the industry's structural challenges.

Outside in winter conditions.

3

The Heavy Hand of the Business Roundtable

Not all owners and contractors welcomed the collaborative relationship with the building trades unions. There were numerous owner attempts to wrest control of the labor markets over the course of the first half of the twentieth century—most notably the "American Plan" of the 1920s—but the typical limited-focus, one-off building project mentality served as a barrier to the long-term, well-resourced, concentrated, adversarial, and often violent campaigns routinely conducted against other segments of the labor movement. Owners/developers had to justify to lenders why taking on the tough slog of challenging a reliable, if perhaps costly, source of skilled labor outweighed the short-term priority of getting a building erected and occupied and loans repaid. Planning beyond the next schedule deadline, requisition, and partial payment was not a characteristic feature of construction management. A successful war waged against construction labor would have required immediate sacrifices to achieve long-term objectives.

From the owners' perspective, union influence had finally blossomed into a full-fledged crisis by the late 1960s. An article in the December 1968 issue of *Fortune* described building trades unions as "the most powerful oligopoly in the American economy" and blamed the "passive stance of management" as enabling the unions' stranglehold.[1] For twenty-five years building trades workers had achieved steadily ascending wage levels and wanted more still. Nearly one-fourth of all worker days on strike in 1969–70 occurred in the construction industry. In 1972, construction accounted for one-half of all major strikes.[2] The combination of a building boom, the strike wave, and labor shortages due to the number of young men serving overseas in Vietnam resulted in a series of particularly high union wage increases.

In 1970, Edwin Gott of U.S. Steel, claimed that the most serious problem affecting the overall economy was "the effect of the high costs of labor settlements in the construction industry."[3] In 1969, a group of executives from most of the nation's largest corporations—that is, repeat clients or "users" of the construction industry—formed the Construction Users Anti-Inflation Roundtable, to be renamed the Business Roundtable in 1972. Prior to becoming one of the country's principal corporate voices on national policy discussions, the organization's founding goal was to reduce inflationary building costs and rein in what was perceived as excessive union power in the building trades, namely, the power to elevate wages and to control the day-to-day culture of the job site.[4] These owners wanted to realign the interests and power relations between owners, contractors, and unions. They rebelled at what they viewed as an excessively cozy relationship between contractors and unions.

The long-standing and relatively stable system of labor relations may have been effective in terms of developing and retaining a skilled workforce, but owners chafed at the power ceded to the unions. Unlike their manufacturing counterparts, construction users were not focused on introducing advances in mechanization. Instead, they adopted a laser-like emphasis on creating an environment in which construction employers pledged obeisance to the client who was paying the bills rather than the labor organizations that represented the employees. The Roundtable issued a series of reports titled "More Construction for the Money," in which they bemoaned the "inordinate fragmentation" of the industry. In the absence of cost-effective management systems, the reports concluded that "the big losers are owners."[5] Referring to itself as an educational mechanism, the Roundtable sought to rationalize the industry along the lines of conventional large-scale corporations. Winton Blount, head of one of the nation's larger general contracting firms, helped found the Roundtable and held several other high-profile positions, including the presidency of the U.S. Chamber of Commerce and Postmaster General in the Nixon administration. In 1968, he described construction labor relations as "chaotic at best" and went on to suggest that "despotic or unbelievable may be better terms."[6] Blount and his colleagues argued that foremen, superintendents, and even the principals of subcontracting firms demonstrated more loyalty to the union than to the general contractor or the owner.

The Roundtable's aim was to place supervision firmly in management's hands, both in the executive office and on the job site. The Roundtable proposed a restructuring of industry responsibilities. At the time of the reports' publication, the traditional self-performing general contractor system dominated the industry. General contractors typically employed crews of carpenters, laborers, and masons and often owned numerous pieces of excavating equipment. The mechanical work on a project—electrical, plumbing, pipefitting, and so forth—was usually farmed out to specialty subcontractors, but the general contractors still provided much of the overall labor force on a construction site. Roundtable leaders believed this system produced higher costs. Not only did powerful building trades unions drive up wages, but contractors had no real incentive to reduce costs and, on the contrary, often had incentives to increase them. A 1977 textbook on construction management pointed out that it was common practice to bid jobs low and make money through add-ons. "In negotiations for changes and extras, the general contractor tends to side with subcontractors against the owner," the authors wrote. "He, after all, will probably work with the same subcontractors on another job, while his commitments to the owner beyond the contract may be negligible."[7]

The shift away from the traditional general contractor to a construction manager model was a response to owner complaints. After all, the owners paid the bills. Like the earlier model of general contracting, the reinvented construction manager negotiated a contract with the owner, handled all the subcontracts, and was responsible for coordinating the flow and outcome of the project. But the construction manager now worked for a fee rather than a lump sum bid. The burden of risk—the ability to make or lose money on the basis of a fixed estimate—and the responsibility of managing crews had been shifted to the multiple subcontractors and created, at times, an oppositional relationship between the former partners. The new construction managers were essentially service companies that solicited clients and marketed products produced by subcontractors. Between 1967 and 1997, general contractors' share of direct construction worker employment fell from 35% to 24% of the labor force whereas specialty subcontractors' portion increased from 48% to 63%.[8] By the end of the twentieth century, the change was well established. A 2000 textbook on project management suggested that the era in which general contractors "performed significant amounts of work with their own forces is largely over."[9]

The construction manager was now an extension of the owners' vision and wallet. In some ways, the restructuring of the construction industry over the past fifty years paralleled changes in industrial relations across industries. Corporations shed traditional legal and social obligations to employees as they shifted from the long-standing role as the primary source of employment to a growing utilization of and reliance on supply chains, vendors, and multitier systems of subcontractors in industries as varied as hospitality, warehousing, retail, and manufacturing. The shift from general contracting to construction management was similar to a fissuring business strategy that transferred the coordination of employment relations and product standards to a multitude of franchisees, labor brokers, and other third-party managers—all in the name of seeking freedom from direct responsibilities for a workforce and the resultant cost savings.[10]

Construction was sheltered from many of the more notorious managerial innovations of the 1980s, such as globalization, automation, and outsourcing, because off-shoring the production of complex physical structures posed too many insurmountable logistical challenges. While the Roundtable proposed the adoption of modern techniques from aerospace and defense management systems, they were less interested in technological advances than in simply clarifying the primacy of the owner in the construction hierarchy. If President Reagan's firing of the air traffic controllers in 1981 served as a message to the public that the federal government was neither sympathetic nor neutral in its stance toward organized labor, the Business Roundtable's effective campaign against the building trades unions was the private sector's "canary in the coal mine" memo that even the most entrenched wing of the labor movement could be weakened.

The Roundtable's powerful affiliates had the resources to launch a comprehensive long-term campaign to limit union impact at a time when the bulk of the nation's major projects were still built with unionized workers. When planning privately funded capital projects, many of the member corporations chose to hire non-union general contractors as a means of subsidizing and promoting the open shop—or non-union—sector. They supported the expansion of the Associated Builders and Contractors (ABC) as a counterweight to the Associated General Contractors (AGC) and other existing employer associations dominated by contractors with collective bargaining agreements. The AGC dated back to 1918 and had long served as the primary voice of the industry. The upstart ABC was founded in 1950 but did not have a significant footprint until the Roundtable propped it up as an anti-union vehicle in the halls of Congress and state legislatures around the country.

The Roundtable and its allies developed a political agenda initially attempting, but failing, to deliver sufficient congressional votes to repeal or weaken the Davis-Bacon Act, a 1931 law that mandated hourly wage rates (usually the union scale in a given locality) on federally financed construction projects. Instead, they successfully supported efforts to repeal state prevailing wage—or "mini-Davis-Bacon"—laws. Davis-Bacon covered public buildings or public works supported by federal dollars, while the state prevailing wage laws applied to all the state and municipal-funded public school, town library, and fire and police station projects. The union rates on those sites served as the standard for the entire industry. Legislative or referendum-based campaigns to accomplish repeal gained momentum in the 1970s and 1980s. Nine states repealed these laws during the decade beginning in 1979. Another wave took place in recent years as six more states have enacted repeals since 2015. As of 2022, twenty-four states never had or now have no prevailing wage law.[11] Economist Peter Philips has argued convincingly that in construction, the attack on state prevailing wage laws was the functional equivalent of deregulatory legislation and rule making in trucking, airlines, and other industries.[12]

Just as significantly, lobbyists were able to convince Congress to enact Section 530 of the Revenue Act of 1978. Congressional supporters argued that the Internal Revenue Service (IRS) had inappropriately increased vigilance in the enforcement of employment tax laws over the previous decade. Companies that treated workers as independent contractors complained that the IRS was imposing costly reclassification penalties that created past and future liabilities. The term misclassification has multiple meanings but, in this context, it refers to the practice of inappropriately treating employees as independent contractors. Section 530, and additional amendments in 1982, granted a "safe harbor," i.e., protection from penalties, to employers that had a "reasonable basis" for treating workers as non-employees. Congress explicitly defined reasonableness as the standard when the use of independent contractors was a "long-standing recognized practice of a significant segment" of an industry. From the perspective of a formerly compliant construction contractor, Section 530 gave a green light to reclassifying its workforce based on the argument that a significant segment of its competitors may already have been treating their workers as non-employees.[13]

The consequences of Section 530 still resonate. Thirty-six years after the law's passage, former IRS commissioner Steve Miller described the bill as "Congress' slap at the IRS when the IRS was active in this area."[14] A 2009 Government Accountability Office report cited additional IRS staffers who claimed that the safe harbor was a major reason they could not examine many suspected cases of misclassification.[15] In 2014, IRS revenue officer Dean Prodromos told a reporter that promising cases frequently hit a wall once referred up the chain of command. He claimed that he would routinely receive a "blunt, if cryptic-sounding, message: 'Safe harbor.'" Prodromos went on to say, "It's gotten widely [sic] out of control with the result of Section 530. It's the Wild West out there."[16]

The anti-union political agenda proved to be surgical and effective. The assault on state prevailing wage laws eliminated an industry wage standard. Even though the laws only applied to publicly funded jobs, they established a bar for private work as well. Contractors were reluctant to compensate their workers at different levels depending on the funding source. Paying a higher wage on a high school project than on a downtown office building for the same work would have created confusion, resentment, and problems with morale. The power of the public prevailing wage extended well into the private sector. The neutering of IRS enforcement of employment laws had as great, if not greater, consequences. Opening the doors to misclassifying employees as independent contractors would redefine employment relations in construction. Both developments—the repeal of prevailing wage laws and the increased practice of misclassification—were key components of a downhill slippery slope of reduced compensation and union density.

Speed square, a traditional layout tool.

4

Misclassification as
a Business Model

The Roundtable's political and organizational program created a context for a workplace that enabled the growth of misclassification as an employment strategy. The increased use of independent contractors in construction was a crucial part of the broader breakdown of the system of labor relations during the 1980s. A large swath of corporations in many industries sought to reduce the fixed aspect of labor costs represented by a core workforce and to eliminate implicit employment guarantees by contracting out work more freely, developing subcontracts for business services, and using more part-time, freelance, and temporary workers. At the time, economist Audrey Freedman argued that the practice of relying on contingent workers might not have been a new concept, but "using contingent worker and subcontracting techniques to gain more adaptability and flexibility—to gain power for rapid downsizing and cost cutting—is what is new."[1]

Using independent contractors on building projects similarly limited risk and shifted the employment burden through the expansion of multitier subcontracting. Construction differed from other major industries in that it already depended on a long-standing system of subcontracting, which simplified restructuring efforts by simply extending an existing set of contractual relations. Further, the political and legislative developments of the 1970s and 1980s had opened the floodgates for the evolution of a new business model. Stan Marek, CEO of Houston-based Marek, one of the largest interior systems contractors in the South, termed Section 530 as "by far the most abused change in the history of the IRS."[2] He attributed the destruction of the union sector of the building industry in Texas in the 1980s to the growth of independent contracting enabled by the amended tax code.

The newly emboldened non-union contractors opted to lower labor costs by compensating tradesmen as independent contractors even though their daily tasks and methods of work remained unchanged. Workers no longer filled out the standard W-4 form when hired. Instead, their employer sent them a year-end 1099-MISC form and left the tax consequences to each individual worker. According to Marek, Texas firms demanded that workers sign a waiver saying they would provide their own insurance for work-related injuries. When workers were hurt on the job, they went to local emergency rooms where they were considered indigent, as few had the resources to purchase a health insurance policy.[3] The Sheet Metal and Air Conditioning Contractors' National Association (SMACNA), a union employer group, described misclassification as "an epidemic in the construction industry."[4] Though the Associated Builders and Contractors (ABC) fiercely opposed periodic legislative attempts to repeal Section 530, responsible non-union employers such as Marek complained that it was becoming "impossible for companies like ours that play by the rules to compete" when, by his estimation, half the workers were hired as independent contractors.[5]

The motivation driving the elimination of employee status was simple. The various state and federal tax and insurance obligations associated with hiring employees constituted a significant portion of total compensation costs. The ability to eliminate as much as 30% or more of labor costs by simply reclassifying a company's workforce as independent contractors was a clever and effective method to gain a competitive edge over other contractors who continued to bear the burden of required mandates. Like employers in other industries, construction contractors abandoned the obligations to pay their share of unemployment, Social Security, and Medicare taxes (as well as earned sick time in some states) by redefining employees as independent contractors.

Construction firms had an additional incentive. They shed the burden of workers' compensation insurance policies that carry above-average premiums because of the risks inherent in the dangerous construction industry. For example, a typical Boston union concrete subcontractor currently pays 35% of a carpenter's wages in taxes and insurances.[6] A company that employs ironworkers engaged in the hazardous erection of high-rise structural steel would be faced with still higher workers' compensation premiums. Unionized companies are contractually unable to adopt misclassification schemes because collective bargaining agreements require that their workforce be treated as employees. For non-union contractors that already pay lower wages than their union counterparts and provide few, if any, benefits, however, the temptation to realize significant labor cost savings and to further extend the compensation gap and competitive edge became virtually irresistible.

Legitimate independent contractors and small firms do and always have existed in the world of construction. The plumber who visits homes to install a new water heater or kitchen sink may well run a genuine small business—scheduling appointments, providing estimates, carrying out the physical labor during the day, and recording financial information at home in the evenings. The 1982 Census of Construction Industries reported that 932,608 of the nation's 1.4 million construction establishments functioned without any employees at all.[7] There was also a tradition in the less formal residential industry of summer help, side jobs, or young people starting in the trades—an electrician's helper, a member of a wood-framing crew—being paid by check without deductions and receiving a 1099 form at the end of the year. Frequently, individual workers have not been considered real employees in the trades unless and until they had indicated a career commitment to the trade and the employer. The emergence of misclassification as a broader phenomenon, however, is associated with the now more common use of independent contractor trades workers on large-scale apartment, commercial, institutional, and industrial buildings. No longer confined to building backyard decks or even single-family homes in suburbia, workers classified as independent contractors have become a regular presence on multi-million-dollar projects working for sizable construction employers.

The legal definition of what constitutes an independent contractor is hotly contested. The conventional understanding is that a worker is presumed to be an employee if she or he is operating under the direction and control of another, but the exact definition varies depending on the geographical and legal jurisdiction. At the federal level, the IRS has a twenty-factor test and the Fair Labor Standards Act, enacted in 1938, uses six criteria to determine if an individual is a legitimate independent contractor. Every state has its own statutory definition and, often, slightly contradictory definitions between regulatory agencies within the same state depending on when the enabling legislation was written. The ABC test is the clearest. It presumes workers to be employees unless they are free from another's direction and control, perform services outside the employer's usual course of business, and customarily engage in that trade, occupation, or profession. The test's presumption of employee status sets the bar high. These varied definitions are sufficiently ambiguous to have generated a cottage industry of employment professionals looking for loopholes.

The shades of gray can be difficult to distinguish in some occupations and industries but, for all its seeming chaos, construction operates with a relatively clear organizational structure. Owners arrive at an agreement with general contractors/construction managers to handle all on-site activity. The general contractor executes a series of subcontracts with specialty trades contractors that employ the bulk of the trades workers on the project. The project manager and superintendent coordinate the various subcontractors whose foremen, in turn, supervise workers carrying out the day-to-day tasks. The concept of independent contracting should not even enter the equation. There is no room for a worker to operate independently from the chain of command. It simply would not work. Self-direction is the antithesis of co-ordination, the single most important element of the successful execution of a construction project.

The lure of cost savings in a highly competitive environment drove non-union subcontractors to embrace the use of misclassification. While the supposedly independent craft worker's routine may have appeared to be identical to that of an employee, the chances of an employer being caught and punished were minimal, particularly in the lightly regulated private construction market. Construction employers made a simple cost-benefit analysis and reached a business decision. The likelihood of regulatory enforcement was negligible and, even if sanctioned, the tax and insurance savings generally outweighed potential penalties. Individual workers, however, bore significant costs associated with misclassification. Anyone who is misclassified foregoes basic rights available to employees by law. In addition to being responsible for any health and retirement security benefits, the individual loses all legal rights to minimum wage or overtime payments, workers' compensation coverage in case of an on-the-job injury, unemployment benefits in case of layoff, anti-discrimination defenses, and the right to form a union. Contractors sometimes chose to sweeten the pot, for example, by offering one hourly rate if the worker insisted on being an employee or a slightly higher one upon acceptance of independent contractor status. The actual work was the same, but the short-term gain of additional hourly pay sometimes was sufficient inducement for the worker to sacrifice legal protections, and the contractor still realized net savings.

In one of the rare examples of successful prosecution, the U.S. Department of Labor entered into consent judgments in 2015 with sixteen defendants covering over 1,000 construction workers in the Southwest who had been improperly classified as independent contractors. The DOL case revealed that the targeted companies required workers to become "member/owners" of limited liability companies (LLCs) in order to continue building houses in Utah and Arizona. One day they were functioning as employees and the next day they were performing the same work on the same jobsites for the same companies as independent contractors. The investigation began in southern

Utah and then moved to Arizona after the passage of state legislation in Utah required LLCs to provide workers' compensation and unemployment insurance to their "members." In response, the defendants moved their operations south to avoid legal jeopardy. In 2013, Paul Johnson Drywall entered into a contract with Arizona Tract, one of the defendants, to supply drywall labor. Under their agreement, the only service Arizona Tract offered was to assume responsibility for former Johnson employees and classify them as member/owners. The DOL consent judgment included back wages for workers, civil penalties, the payment of applicable federal, state, and local taxes, and the re-classification of workers as employees with all the protections provided by the federal Fair Labor Standards Act.[8]

Consultants around the country provided counsel to construction employers who sought to cut costs through this newly refined mechanism. Legal and accounting firms sustained a specialized practice by writing hundreds of articles and convening seminars to teach clients how to take advantage of the safe harbor provision. As an example, Attorney Simon Leeming opened a small law firm in southern New Hampshire in 1988. The mainstay of his practice quickly became a group of subcontractors who hoped to take advantage of the opportunities in the growing drywall sector of the industry. As a product, drywall (also known by the brand name Sheetrock) had been introduced to the industry in the early part of the twentieth century. Ads in pre-WWII trade journals portrayed pipe-smoking carpenters in white overalls leisurely hammering 4 X 8 sheets of drywall with individual nails. By the second half of the century, metal stud framing and drywall hanging had become a major subtrade as the method of choice for creating interior and exterior partitions in buildings. The speed of installation (aided by the introduction of electric and now cordless screw guns) rendered the new subspecialty unappealing to traditional generalist carpenters who looked down on the go-go production nature of the work and left it to others to fill the vacuum. In New England, that void was filled by a generation of French-Canadians who had crossed the border during the 1980s to take advantage of job prospects. Individual construction trades have always had a strong ethnic affiliation and this cohort, bound by ties of language and communities of origin, gravitated as a group toward the opportunities afforded in drywall. Many had started their careers as employees in Quebec, a province with stringent labor laws, but, in the spirit of the prevailing winds of United States employment law, Leeming, like other construction management attorneys, instructed employers to treat this workforce as independent contractors. The goal was to create a paper-intensive, legally defensible wall of protection. At

Leeming's direction, clients insisted "that each independent contractor signed an independent contract outlining the duties towards taxes, unemployment, Workers' Comp, and all the other indicia of employment."[9]

Leeming's small-scale approach was mirrored across the country. The American Bar Association's Construction Lawyers Guide even developed a five-page boilerplate independent contractor agreement for construction contractors.[10] Though the character of the work remained unchanged in terms of the underlying criteria of direction and control, many courts accepted the existence of this type of document as solely determinant. As an example, a Pennsylvania carpenter named Mulzet was hired in 1998 by drywall contractor R.L. Reppert. According to subsequent court documents, the company supplied all the necessary power tools and Mulzet brought his hand tools—standard practice in the industry. The federal judge in the case acknowledged that Mulzet performed the same work as company employees, was paid hourly as were company employees, and his work was assigned and evaluated by the same supervisors. But Reppert had required Mulzet to sign an independent contractor agreement as a condition of employment and, as a result, the judge ruled that the document alone "tips the scales decidedly in favor of the conclusion that Mulzet was an independent contractor."[11]

The practice of classifying putative employees as independent contractors has occasioned a contemporary national policy discussion as a result of its widespread adoption by gig economy firms. Today rideshare and other platform companies justify the classification in terms of supposed worker independence, flexibility, and entrepreneurialism. The use of independent contractors in construction, however, long predated the advent of the gig economy. Mulzet was one of hundreds of thousands and the numbers have only grown since. There were no rationalizations in terms of heightened worker autonomy. There were no euphemisms about worker liberty. It was simply a labor cost-cutting measure in a highly competitive industry by employers who made a decision that altering or defying employment laws made business sense. The competitive advantage accrued from lowering costs illegally far outweighed the minimal likelihood of possible penalties.

Staircase under construction.

5

Immigration, Payroll Fraud, and the Underground Economy

The practice of misclassification was accelerated by the passage of the 1986 comprehensive Immigration Reform and Control Act (IRCA), a bill intended to stem the flow of migrants crossing the Mexican border into the United States. Many business associations opposed IRCA because it contained penalties against employers who knowingly hired undocumented workers. The provision was intended to pressure employers to abandon the practice of exploiting the lack of citizenship status as a means of reducing labor costs. The attempt was largely unsuccessful since the legal standard of "knowingly" was difficult to prove, but businesses found an additional unintended consequence of the legislation. Since the employer sanctions were only triggered if the new hire was an employee, one obvious conclusion was to hire new workers as independent contractors instead. In a 1987 Associated General Contractors (AGC) Q&A sheet on the new legislation, one of the questions posed was: "What if I decide just to give up and have no one in my business other than independent contractors and leased employees?"[1] The answer was self-evident.

Even before IRCA, immigration and misclassification had become inextricably linked. As early as 1984, Rice University economist Donald Huddle claimed that one-third of all commercial construction jobs in the Houston area were filled by undocumented workers from Mexico, Central America, and South America. His study suggested that these workers were being treated as independent contractors so that employers could avoid paying taxes.[2] According to the many Pew Research Center studies on immigration, the proportion of Hispanic male workers in construction increased four times as fast as the increase of white male workers between 1990 and 2000.[3] By the end of 2006, nearly one-third of recently arrived, foreign-born Hispanics were working in construction, predominantly in the South and, to a slightly lesser extent, in the West.[4] In Los Angeles County, the percentage of Latinos working in construction jobs climbed from 24% in 1980 to 70% in 2015.[5] The Center for Migration Studies and the Migration Policy Institute estimated 1.7 million undocumented workers in Texas alone in 2014, 24% of whom worked in construction.[6] Undocumented immigrants made up 15% of the total national construction workforce, outnumbering immigrant workers with valid working papers.[7]

Construction continues to employ the largest share of undocumented workers of any major industry category. The Workers Defense Project has conducted two studies on construction workers' conditions—one in Texas and one across the South. Their findings demonstrated that half of the workforce in Texas was foreign born and that, in six southern states, nearly one third was undocumented.[8] In certain non-licensed trades with a tradition of piecework—drywall, ceilings, wood framing, roofing, bricklaying, floorcovering, painting, and taping—the numbers were even higher. The lack of acceptable immigration documentation exposed these workers to a work life characterized by unsafe conditions, poverty-level payments, and wage theft. More than 40% of the surveyed group in Texas reported that they routinely experienced nonpayment of overtime and, in many cases, nonpayment of any wages.

The tectonic shift in construction workforce demographics depended on a steady labor supply chain. The people who recruited workers and their families to cross the border illegally were referred to as coyotes, a colloquial term dating back to the nineteenth century. The coyote system of smuggling groups of people for a fee was well suited for the multitier subcontracting system of construction. Coyotes expanded their role to become labor brokers, using smart phones with hundreds of contacts to function as informal hiring halls, supplying subcontractors with workers wherever and whenever they were needed. The relationship between subcontractors and labor brokers also provided a shield against legal liability unless overburdened regulators and auditors took on the herculean task of applying joint employer or criminal conspiracy standards to connect the two entities.

Frank Gomez worked briefly as a labor broker in Georgia and Florida. Because he spoke Spanish, he was able to provide organizational direction for the growing number of Mexican trades workers in the South. He worked as a lower tier subcontractor to drywall firms that held contracts with general contractors. The lead subcontractor had employees, typically white men, performing the layout and framing tasks, while Gomez worked with other labor brokers to bring in crews to hang and finish the drywall. The brokers and workers alike were paid on a piece work basis and were classified as independent contractors. "There were so many crooks in the industry," says Gomez now, "that it was an eye opener. You learn more in a bad company than a good one, because you learn all the bad things not to do."[9]

Labor brokers have developed complex schemes to evade obligations, particularly the high cost of workers compensation insurance premiums. Most states require contracts between construction managers/general contractors and their subcontractors to include a certificate of insurance (COI) as proof of coverage. A 2012 Florida Division of Insurance Fraud investigation revealed a pattern in which labor brokers worked with facilitators associated with money service or check cashing businesses. The facilitator would rent a shell company with a legally registered corporate identity to a broker who then applied for a policy with a minimal payroll. Once the insurance agent issued a COI, the facilitator rented the same shell entity to other unrelated labor brokers for a similar purpose. This mechanism allowed a shell called E South Construction that claimed just four employees to purchase 450 COIs and earn over $11 million.[10]

In 2011, Jaime Juache was supplying labor to interior systems subcontractor Roswell Drywall LLC of Georgia on the $600 million Music City Convention Center project in Nashville. A recorded exchange between the labor broker and a journalist pretending to apply for work stripped bare any pretense of decent wages and legality.

Q [REPORTER]: "How much do you pay by the hour?"
A [JUACHE]: "$13 an hour."
Q: "Any overtime?"
A: "No."
Q: "Do I need my Social Security number?"
A: "No, use any number."
Q: "How do I deal with taxes?"
A: "I'll give you a 1099, then you're responsible for taxes."
Q: "Only $13 you pay?"
A: "Yeah it's the maximum I can pay for experienced people on the job."[11]

Problematic contractors are often referred to as "frequent flyers" since those who pay low wages and skirt legal obligations frequently cut corners on quality and safety as well. Nashville's strong economy created a context for a dramatic increase in dangerous conditions. A report in *The Tennessean* determined that sixteen construction workers died in the Nashville metropolitan area during 2016 and 2017, the deadliest two-year stretch in three decades. Half of the deceased workers were Latino and nearly two-thirds died from falls because they had no harnesses or other basic safety devices.[12] In 2020, sixteen-year-old Gustavo Ramirez was working with his older brother on scaffolding high in the air on a La Quinta Hotel project. His brother heard a noise, turned, and watched as Gustavo became one more fatality statistic of a construction worker without a harness. Investigators summoned to the site initially indicated they were unable to determine who was the responsible employer as the site's general contractor and subcontractors shifted blame on each other. Karla Campbell, an attorney representing the Ramirez family, argued that type of confusion was not a new problem, just another instance of a situation where construction entities can subcontract with "another entity or even a sham entity."[13]

The following year, Councilmember Sandra Sepulveda filed a bill that would have raised Nashville's standards for awarding construction contracts, emphasizing workplace safety and fair payment and compensation. Her bill incentivized contractors by allowing the procurement board to grant higher scores to bidders who invested in training, provided health benefits, maintained clean workplace safety records, and participated in apprenticeship programs. "It's important that we advocate for people just like Gustavo who didn't have that protection," said Sepulveda, "and didn't have their contractors and their bosses looking out for their safety." Unfortunately, the Tennessee state legislature quickly passed a bill prohibiting local governments from favoring companies that offered worker benefits in the procurement process, another instance of red state legislatures pre-empting blue city legislation. Angered by the "gutting" of her bill, Sepulveda lashed out at the legislators: "They're going to listen to interest groups and lobbyists and the last thing they're thinking about is workers."[14]

Twenty years earlier, at the western end of the state, labor broker David Cantu pleaded guilty to federal charges of conspiracy, money laundering, and tax evasion stemming from his role in providing drywall carpenters to a contractor working on a FedEx headquarters project in Memphis. Cantu had referred 148 undocumented workers from Texas to the site, many of whom were crowded into apartments that he leased. The carpenters typically worked fifty-six to sixty-four hours per week without overtime pay and, according to the U.S. Attorney's filing, Cantu had forced the workers to sign independent contractor agreements under the threat of termination. During the trial, Cantu cited the agreements as a defense and further argued that he was not responsible for the workers' legal work authorization status.[15]

Though Cantu's strategy failed in this particular case, the growth of the immigrant workforce had begun to undermine the rationale for a paper-intensive legal approach to misclassification. If a question of uncertain citizenship status already existed, many employers and labor brokers began to wonder why they should bother with lengthy legal documents and 1099 forms. Entering the world of the underground economy through a system of paychecks without deductions or straight cash was a simpler and more cost-effective method of compensation. The transition from independent contracting with a legal paper trail to off-the-books unreported cash compensation further complicated regulatory options. Active enforcement agencies had been able to track the advance of independent contracting by monitoring the issuance of 1099 forms. But the descent into the underground economy and under-the-table payments posed new and nearly insurmountable obstacles. Studies have indicated that for every construction worker issued a 1099 instead of the appropriate W2 form, at least two more were paid off the books.[16] The challenge of measuring, let alone regulating, employer behavior when the entire system of compensation was unrecorded, stymied investigators accustomed to building cases through documentation.

In 1996, the Department of Homeland Security introduced the E-Verify system to block the employment of undocumented workers. The new system failed. In many cases, the result was a boom in the black market for stolen, rented, or fake social security cards or, in the case of a document mismatch, to drive workers further into the shadows of the underground economy. Rebuilding the Gulf Coast after Hurricane Katrina enhanced the power of the labor broker system, by then a consistent source of desperately needed labor across the South. On a 2015 project in Houston built by one of the area's largest general contractors with a reputation for quality and safety, one of the major subcontractors supplemented its hourly workforce through a staffing company. Forty-five of the sixty-member crew worked for the labor broker. They were undocumented and earned $14 an hour and received no overtime pay, whereas the fifteen documented workers were paid $22 an hour for identical work. The labor broker did not provide workers' compensation insurance and, to the contrary, told the workers if they tried to obtain coverage, they would be deported.[17] Legal employment has become the exception on construction sites in the region.

The growing use of undocumented workers coupled with the practice of payroll fraud and wage theft spread from the South to the rest of the country in the early 2000s. By 2010, for example, a New York Building Congress analysis claimed that 45% of the city's trades workers were not U.S. citizens, and a Fiscal Policy Institute study suggested that the level of payroll fraud was particularly acute in the city's affordable housing industry, in which fully two-thirds of the workforce either worked as independent contractors or were paid off-the-books.[18] Further north, Management Attorney Leeming noticed that his French-Canadian clients in New England were being supplanted by a system of Hispanic workers working for labor brokers who were "less compliant with the law."[19]

Employers took pains to ensure that the new workforce operated in the shadows of the industry. In 2007, the New England Regional Council of Carpenters filed a petition for an election to represent carpenters working for National Carpentry Contractors, one of the region's largest nonunion wood-framing companies. National Carpentry had erected thousands of units of mid-rise apartments in Massachusetts and Connecticut for national publicly traded merchant builders such as Avalon Bay Communities. Dozens of carpenters worked on every National Carpentry job site under the direction of a company superintendent. Yet, in response to the union's petition, owner John Kirk asserted that he "never employed any employees." In a particularly twisted legal analysis, the Regional Office of the National Labor Relations Board concluded that "the fact that the Employer may have exercised some supervisory authority over the employees . . . or that it may have paid employees directly, or participated in their hiring, or set their initial wage rates, or provided them with tools does not, however, provide conclusive evidence that it was the Employer alone who employed them." Kirk told the Board that the real employers were a group of 14 subcontractors. When the Board sent subpoenas to the addresses of the subcontractors, all were returned "undeliverable."[20]

Ricardo Batres, a Minnesota labor broker, was arrested in 2018 on charges of labor trafficking and under-reporting workers compensation insurance information. According to a court filing, Batres seized on the vulnerability of his undocumented workforce, threatening to call immigration authorities if the workers complained about the submarket wages, long hours without overtime pay, and living quarters with no hot running water. His crews of independent contractors were subjected to unsafe conditions and, in one instance, Batres insisted that a worker get massage therapy after his back was broken by a falling pre-fabricated wall. According to the probable-cause statement in the criminal complaint, the crews lived and worked in fear and shocking conditions.[21]

The U.S. Attorney's Office for the Middle District of Florida has been active in pursuing cases of fraud in construction. In 2021, the office obtained guilty pleas from two facilitators for conspiracy to commit wire fraud and tax fraud. The two men had rented COIs to hundreds of work crews, thus avoiding $3.6 million in insurance premiums.[22] A year later, a plea agreement was reached with Guillermo Inamagua and Mayra Velasquez, a couple who were owners of First Construction and Best Construction, respectively.

In reality, Inamagua and Velasquez were labor brokers who, in addition to falsifying payroll figures to avoid workers compensation premiums, provided check cashing services for cash payments to the undocumented workers they had referred to various contractors. Best and First Construction disclaimed responsibility for ensuring that jobsite workers were legally authorized to work in the United States and that required state and federal payroll taxes and insurance premiums were being paid. As a result, the contractors who actually paid these workers' wages and used their services were also able to avoid responsibility as well. According to the U.S. Attorney's calculations, these misrepresentations caused a loss to the IRS of nearly $6.5 million in unpaid payroll taxes.[23]

These cases represent the tip of a growing iceberg. While both civil and criminal actions against these labor brokers and shell companies are welcome, the upper-tier contractors who ultimately benefit from the fraud are rarely held accountable. Ricardo (last name withheld) worked as a project manager and estimator for several non-union contractors. In an interview with a union representative, he argued that the lower tier subcontractors and brokers are often forced into illegal practices by the very nature of the industry's dynamics. They are typically handed a contract by the general contractor or upper-tier subcontractor offering a sum for a particular scope of work yet are rarely provided access to the project's blueprints or job specifications. When changes are ordered—a routine occurrence as jobs progress—the upper-tier subcontractor can falsely indicate that the extra work was simply part of the original scope, thereby squeezing the lower-tier subcontractor's profit margin and pocketing the additional revenue. Ricardo suggested that without access to job documents, the lower-tier subcontractors regularly face a Hobson's choice of running out of money or shortchanging their workers.[24] Both scenarios occur frequently. Matt Capece is a long-time union staffer who spends his time trying to motivate regulatory agencies to take on ever more cases of payroll fraud. "You can feel some satisfaction that a few bad actors were nailed, but the contractors that use these services remain untouched," comments Capece. "As long as law enforcement focuses on the lower tier, they are destined to play whack-a-mole while these schemes solidify control of markets they dominate and take control of others."[25]

The Covid era only reinforced the connection between misclassification, immigration, and unsafe working conditions. In union areas, contractors had the same struggles with masks and vaccination mandates as other employers, largely dependent on an owner's wishes and the policies of the local jurisdiction. Most unions weighed in, providing education for members to make informed choices. Construction workers as a whole repeatedly polled higher than the national average in terms of vaccine hesitancy, but in predominantly non-union areas, the lack of an organized worker voice and proactive safety measures drove up infection rates, particularly among low-waged Latino construction workers. In June of 2020, Dr. Betsey Tilson, North Carolina's Director of the Department of Health and Human Services, called construction sites high-risk settings. She cited Durham County, where Latinos represented nearly 61% of all confirmed COVID-19 cases while accounting for just 14% of the population. The greatest number of cases, she pointed out, were found among construction workers.[26]

How widespread has payroll fraud become? It is difficult to measure accurately the prevalence and severity of misclassification in construction. Independent contractors have a high incidence of not reporting earnings to state and federal tax authorities, and the debate over what differentiates conventional employee status from genuine independent contracting clouds the clarity of the data. More important, off-the-books compensation is, by its very nature, unrecorded and unreported and therefore challenging to quantify. Few regulatory agencies have the resources to do extensive forensic audits of the multiple subcontracting tiers that might reveal the extent of both misclassification and cash compensation. Reliance on impacted workers as a source of data on the degree of payroll fraud is problematic since studies show that workers who are the least likely to voice complaints are often immigrants who tend to be in workplaces with a higher degree of informal work arrangements.[27]

Studies on the subject, nonetheless, indicate payroll fraud of either type is an alarming problem. In 2004, the Harvard Labor and Worklife Program issued one of the first reports to quantify the impact of misclassification and argued that the scheme had broad negative public policy consequences. The report demonstrated that taxpayers were paying the price for the growing use of independent contractors even in a state with an above average rate of unionization and regulatory activity. Using data from the Massachusetts Division of Unemployment Assistance (DUA), the authors calculated that 14% to 24% of all construction employers misclassified their workers from 2001 to 2003. As a result of misclassification across all industries, the Commonwealth of Massachusetts lost an estimated total of $152 million in uncollected income tax revenues and up to $35 million in unemployment insurance taxes during those years. In addition, insurance companies were deprived of $91 million in unpaid workers' compensation insurance premiums. Based on examination of ten years of DUA records, the study concluded that the prevalence and severity of misclassification had substantially increased over the previous decade.[28]

The Harvard report received widespread publicity and spawned a series of similar studies in California, Colorado, Illinois, Michigan, Minnesota, New Jersey, New York, Tennessee, and other states. The various reports on workers compensation fraud alone show an escalating problem. In 2019, for example, the Tennessee Bureau of Workers' Compensation reported premium losses had jumped by 223 percent.[29] The most recent and comprehensive national study estimated conservatively that in 2017, between 12.4% and 20.5% of the construction industry workforce (1.3 to 2.2 million workers) were either improperly classified as independent contractors or employed informally off-the-books. Depending on worker income assumptions, the study concluded that fraudulent employers may have realized between $6.2 and $17.3 billion in labor cost savings, figures that are the basis of estimates of tax revenues lost annually to state and federal coffers as well as premiums unpaid to workers' compensation insurers.[30]

* * *

Many of the elements of the Business Roundtable's realignment wish list were realized over a remarkably short period of time. The adoption of the construction management model and much of the political, legislative, and regulatory agenda were achieved during the 1970s and 1980s. In many ways, that transformation is complete. Writing in *Fortune* in 1979, Gilbert Burck contrasted the building trades' "impregnable monopoly position" in the late 1960s with their "disorderly retreat" only a decade later. Open shop contractors, he continued, "now plausibly claim to dominate the industry."[31] Similarly, Business Roundtable leader Charles Brown, formerly CEO of Du-Pont, claimed in 1982 that construction had once been "monopolized by the union segment with no apparent alternative in sight." Now, he crowed, "the capitalistic system worked again."[32]

How rapid and complete was the victory? In 1952, economists William Haber and Harold Levinson conducted a survey of sixteen cities to determine how deeply unionism was embedded in the construction industry. Rather than rely on Census data exclusively to evaluate union strength, they used market share as a relevant measuring stick. Census figures rely on self-reporting and can underestimate the significance of union membership since a higher proportion of non-union workers flow in and out of the industry and inflate total numbers. Union members are more likely to make careers out of their craft and are more deeply rooted in the industry. Market share, on the other hand, calculates the percentage of total work that is put in place on a union basis. When figured on a dollar basis, market share can overestimate union influence since bigger projects are more likely to require the larger labor force that unions can provide. Nonetheless, market share can be a more common-sense form of assessing power—that is, how big a role do union workers play in a given community's built environment?

Interestingly, the sixteen cities that Haber and Levinson surveyed did not include major metropolises like New York, Philadelphia, Los Angeles, or San Francisco—all of which had strong building trades unions. They included some big cities, such as Chicago, Detroit, and Boston, but their list also incorporated medium-sized municipalities like Battle Creek, Grand Rapids, and Kalamazoo in Michigan, Buffalo, Cincinnati, and even two cities below the Mason-Dixon line—Charleston, West Virginia, and Charlotte, a town that would never be considered a union stronghold in other industries. Nonetheless, the survey indicated that close to 100% of the commercial, industrial, apartment building, and public works were built by unionized contractors using union labor in all sixteen cities. Even more telling, nearly two-thirds of the residential work was performed by union members. In fact, in Chicago, St. Louis, and Cleveland, Haber and Levinson reported that virtually all of the homebuilding was union built.[33]

The transformation of the world of work in construction was swift and severe. The more standard data on union density confirms the Roundtable claims. The percentage of workers in the construction industry who were union members declined from 42% in 1970 to 22% in 1992. The deterioration of union density lowered compensation throughout the industry. Construction workers—union and non-union combined—experienced a 17% drop in real wages between 1980 and 1992.[34] And the trend only continued. In 1983, the median weekly earnings in the construction trades exceeded the median for all workers by 20%. By 1999, the term labor aristocrat had lost much of its relevance. The pay difference between construction and all other workers had sunk to only 3%.[35] The plunge was so complete that in 2001, Frank Yancey, an executive with open shop Kellogg Brown & Root, the nation's third largest contractor, told his colleagues that "if low pay was a felony, I think most of us would be on death row today."[36]

The willful misclassification of employees as independent contractors, the shift to cash compensation, and the use of a vulnerable undocumented workforce has become the dominant labor model in certain areas of the country—deeply embedded as a result of the construction industry's version of a successful deregulatory agenda. The opportunities in construction work today differ dramatically from a half century ago. The work remains dangerous but, despite the physical demands, construction had long served as an enticing path to the middle class for smart and ambitious young men who could not afford or chose not to attend college. The decline of union density, the resulting deterioration of wage rates, and the presence of payroll fraud and the underground economy has removed that path for some trades workers.

In many parts of the country, construction employers complain that it is nearly impossible to find a sufficient number of capable workers. A recent U.S. Chamber of Commerce report suggests that 92% of commercial contractors describe moderate to high levels of difficulty finding skilled workers,[37] and a Home Builders Institute publication suggests that labor shortages are a key limiting factor for improving both housing inventory and affordability.[38] It has long been the conventional wisdom in the industry that construction is no longer an attractive career option for young people, a development typically attributed to cultural and social factors. Interviewed for an article on construction's career crisis, Brian Turmail of the AGC proposed that this trend began forty to fifty years ago when the country moved from an industrial to a post-industrial, service-based business economy and parents guided their children in the direction of college educations. Greg Sizemore of the ABC concurred, claiming that a four-year degree became the hallmark of family success and working in the trades was for "someone else's kid."[39]

Turmail's suggested timeline may well be correct. The construction industry did indeed begin a transformative change forty to fifty years ago, but the attribution of labor shortages to a shift in societal perception conveniently ignores the crucial reality that reduced compensation and training opportunities degraded the value of the trades as an employment option during that period. Why should a young man or woman looking for a job choose to handle heavy concrete forms in 100-degree heat to build a foundation for a Texas shopping complex when safer and cleaner sales positions in one of the retail outlets inside the air-conditioned mall pay roughly the same? Union apprenticeship programs rarely have difficulty recruiting applicants to a promising career in which young people can earn while they learn and avoid the onerous weight of student loan debt. In the non-union sector, however, misclassification, low cash compensation, and precarious employment conditions have diminished the appeal of the trades as an attractive career preference. Recently, AGC Chief Economist Ken Simonson had a simple, if obvious,[40] solution to the problem of labor woes: "For contractors to get more workers on board, I think they'll have to raise pay even more."

On a building edge with a safety harness.

6

Technology and the Future
of Construction Work

Technology has been linked to the potential for human liberation for centuries. Writing nearly two hundred fifty years ago in *Wealth of Nations*, the founding text of classical economics, Adam Smith marveled at the power of machines to "facilitate and abridge labour" and allow one to do the work of many. Famed economist John Maynard Keynes, while concerned about the hazards of technological unemployment, predicted in his short but influential 1930 article, "Economic Possibilities for our Grandchildren," a not-too-distant future in which the combination of "science and compound interest" would present man with a new and permanent problem—that is, "how to use his freedom from pressing economic cares, how to occupy the leisure."[1] Today, there is a sizable and growing body of literature on the future of work prophesying that the increasingly rapid pace of innovation will transform the way we earn a living and spend our days. There is even a website, https://willrobotstakemyjob.com, that offers visitors an opportunity to type in their own occupation to get a personalized automation risk probability.

The projections range from utopian to dystopian. Optimists suggest technology will transplant people from the never-ending drudgery of work to a life of leisure filled with free time for painting, poetry, and charitable volunteering. Pessimists foresee a world of disgruntled, displaced workers, social and political upheaval, and a fundamental threat to democracy and individual freedoms. A perspective between the extremes proposes that technology will simultaneously eliminate existing work functions while creating new opportunities, resulting in a new, largely unchanged equilibrium as long as extensive retraining programs are implemented. They argue that disruption has been a constant element of economic development. A 1987 National

Academy of Sciences study claimed that "historically, technological change and productivity growth have been associated with expanding rather than contracting total employment and rising earnings. The future will see little change in this pattern." A 2020 MIT Future of Work Task Force report agreed, pointing out that most of today's jobs did not even exist in 1940.[2]

The projected numbers mirror the extreme variations in outlooks. A frequently cited work by two Oxford University researchers suggested that nearly half of all workers in the United States are at risk of having jobs replaced by automation while the Organisation for Economic Co-operation and Development (OECD) puts the same estimate at fourteen percent. The McKinsey Global Institute landed in the middle, suggesting that while half of all occupations do have the potential to be automated, less than five percent can be automated entirely as most jobs have a limited amount of automatable component activities. And reinforcing the notion of simultaneous job loss and gain, the World Economic Forum maintains that 85 million jobs may be displaced around the globe by 2025 while 97 million new roles may emerge. These moving targets prompted the *MIT Technology Review* to assemble a chart showing findings from eighteen different research teams. The *Review* concluded that there is no consensus: "Predictions range from optimistic to devastating, differing by tens of millions of jobs."[3]

There is general agreement that the industries most susceptible to disruption through automation include manufacturing, transportation, retail or e-commerce, healthcare, warehousing, and logistics. The most frequently mentioned types of vulnerable jobs involve repetitive physical tasks that robots can handle or analytic, research, and administrative duties susceptible to the application of artificial intelligence. Construction tends to be ignored in the future of work literature, although a Bain report did predict productivity gains in construction due to automation amounting to 32% would take place between 2015 and 2030, producing a savings of 12% in operating costs.[4] The pro-labor Midwest Economic Policy Institute estimated that there will likely be one million additional construction trades workers by 2057 but warned that the estimate was based on current technologies and that increased automation would reduce the number.[5]

More commonly, industry observers deride the lack of technological sophistication and have long pigeon-holed construction as old-fashioned and lagging behind their more forward-looking and purposeful colleagues in manufacturing. In the wake of the post-WWII housing boom, the editors of *Fortune* published a cover story titled "The Industry Capitalism Forgot," in which they mocked homebuilding's "feudal character" and "picayune scale."[6] Seventy years later, McKinsey consultants continued the drumbeat, blaming limited productivity improvements on "poor project management and ex-ecution . . . underinvestment in skills development, R&D, and innovation."[7] A 2016 study claimed that labor productivity had dropped since 1968.[8] MIT Professor John Fernandez summed up the conventional wisdom when he wrote: "It is widely believed that construction is the slowest of all industries of such scale in implementing proven, scientifically sound technological innovation."[9]

For many years, speakers at industry conferences and seminars have re-galed their audiences with woeful tales of the deeply ingrained resistance to innovation. PowerPoint presentations often included a chart based on research by Paul Teicholz of Stanford, showing a steady upward progression of economy-wide productivity gains that more than doubled between 1964 and 2004, contrasted to a ten percent decline in construction productivity during that same period.[10] Teicholz's numbers confirmed the impression of a backward industry and prompted eager consultants to promote and peddle a variety of nostrums. Unfortunately, reliable construction data is difficult to assemble—for metrics like productivity, union density, or employment status, among others—perhaps because of the difficulty of drawing statisti-cally valid conclusions for an industry that is segmented, decentralized, and diffuse. Definitive interpretable data collection is challenging.

Even the assumptions about productivity gains and losses are subject to debate. A more nuanced study by economist Steven Allen broke down the era between 1950 and 1978 into two distinct time frames. Using BLS data, Allen told a different story. He found that construction labor productivity grew by nearly fifty percent between 1950 and 1968 but declined by over twenty-one percent during the following decade. The drop could not be explained by corresponding developments in the broader economy. "While productivity continued to grow in most other sectors of the economy between 1968 and 1978, it was falling in construction," reported Allen.[11] Interestingly, the two intervals' opposing trends uncovered by Allen coincide with a peak period of union strength, on the one hand, and the early stages of the organized attack on the building trades unions, on the other. Productivity grew steadily at a time when well-paid union members built most of the country's projects and infrastructure and declined when non-union conditions began to permeate the industry.

There is no shortage of anecdotal war stories about the opposition to change in the curmudgeonly male-dominated construction culture. The inherent insecurity of life in the trades provoked apprehension in the face of power tools and other labor-saving devices. Regardless of the era, trades workers worry about jobs ending and the unpredictability of future employment. As the saying goes, every day on a job is a day closer to layoff. Design mistakes, rework, and added scope were always welcomed since they extended the life of a project. Joseph Emanuello recalled the first time he encountered electric circular saws: "One guy took the Skilsaw on the roof of the building and threw it off. He said, 'The saw's too fast, I'm going to cut by hand.'"[12] The hesitancy to adopt innovation extended to the contractor's office. When John Tocci, fresh out of engineering school, bought an expensive mainframe computer for his multigenerational family general contracting firm in 1983, his owner/father looked at the bulky item and grumbled, "When that freaking thing can lay brick, I'll learn how to use it."[13] Over thirty years later, a firm called Construction Robotics painstakingly developed a bricklaying robot called SAM (short for Semi-Autonomous Mason). SAM is a co-bot, a collaborative robot that works in tandem with rotating crews of masons and laborers who feed the robot bricks and mortar, point the walls, place metal wall ties, and check quality. SAM performed at a booth in a parking lot outside a Bricklayers Union annual national convention. A delegate walked by, took one look at SAM, and scoffed: "If a robot told me where to lay bricks, I think I'd shove it off the scaffold."[14]

Despite all the colorful stories, resistance to new tools and methods has generally been exaggerated. At that same Bricklayers Convention, General President Jim Boland informed the robot's manufacturer that the union officially intended to embrace SAM and told the delegates that the union needed to adapt if it was to survive another 150 years.[15] In 1993, a researcher conducted interviews with tradesmen about their attitudes toward technological innovation. With few exceptions, they welcomed new tools that made the work safer and less physically demanding and, for the most part, their pride in increased production outweighed their fears of displacement.[16] Now, with the onset of the so-called Fourth Industrial Revolution, the pace of change will undoubtedly increase. A 2019 report by Tractica, a technology market intelligence firm, declares that construction is "ripe for disruption" due to its history of technological underdevelopment and predicts that the purchase of construction robots will increase ten-fold by 2025. Gaurav Kikani, vice president of Built Robotics, declares that there will be "an explosion of robotics" over the next two years that will replace the eight-hour workday with automated activity around the clock. A recent global survey indicated that 81% of construction businesses will introduce or increase their use of robotics and automation in the coming decade.[17]

Adam Smith's fascination with machines has continued and been surpassed by the current crop of engineers' and tinkerers' ingenious new inventions. The exuberant enchantment with disruption and innovation may be excessive, but new products are slowly being absorbed into the daily rhythms of the construction industry. Just as the emergence of autonomous passenger vehicles has captured (and occasionally terrified) the public's imagination, the same technology is being applied to heavy equipment machinery. Semi-automatic excavators for grading are already being replaced by fully autonomous bulldozers that can dig trenches, excavate foundations, and grade building pads and roads. If the work is repetitive, the machine can learn from previous activity. The autonomous fleet can be keyboard-operated via a web-based platform. The human operator needs to fuel the machine, grease the equipment, and press go. The International Union of Operating Engineers has formed a partnership with an autonomous heavy equipment manufacturer to train their members to operate these vehicles.[18]

The enthusiasm for autonomous excavators is only topped by high hopes for robots. State-of the-art six-axis articulated robots may have transformed the auto industry, but their stationery character does not work on a construction site. In the controlled environment of an auto plant, parts and materials can be moved into the robot's wheelhouse ready for welding and assembly. A robot that is immobile and cannot adjust to the rough ground and multistory nature of a building project is functionally useless. Layout and documentation appear to be basic tasks that can be more easily automated. A startup called RCML has developed Oliver, a four-wheeled mobile robot that uses a 3D laser scanner to map the structure as it goes up to ensure that the various elements of the design have been properly placed. Oliver can also spray paint lines on the ground for layout for the trades workers that follow. Doxel is promoting a lidar-equipped robot, and Boston Dynamics is marketing Spot the robot dog for $74,500 to image capture and laser scan. Company representatives claim Spot can autonomously walk, open doors, and handle uneven terrain. The Husky A200 can carry tools and materials around the job site.[19]

There are larger and more clearly labor-displacing robots as well. Canvas, a San Francisco–based company, has developed a drywall taping and finishing machine that combines a seventeen-foot-high scissor lift with a robotic arm. Human tenders operate the robot, which can apply paper tape, spray joint compound, and sand for a high-level finish on sheetrocked walls, reducing a seven-day job to just two. Drywall framing, hanging, and taping are disproportionately responsible for musculoskeletal disorders and, as a result, the Painters Union has not actively resisted the introduction of taping robots. In fact, Canvas is signatory to a collective bargaining agreement with the union's District Council 16 in California. The council's business manager characterizes the machines as "making the work itself safer and reducing the strain on the body."[20]

Drones equipped with 3D mapping capabilities can buzz high above construction sites and create models of work completed, allowing managers to monitor daily, weekly, and monthly progress. A Kansas company's drones fly two hundred feet in the air using artificial intelligence and algorithms to spot defects and problems on bridge work below. The drone's camera's infrared sensors can detect electromagnetic radiation and heat fluctuation that indicate areas of stress. Advanced Construction Robotics produces a reinforcing bar–tying robot, called Tybot, to secure rebar on bridge decks. A University of Michigan team announced the development of a drone to fly to a designated location, generate enough force to nail down roof shingles, and move to the next spot. In November of 2021, the New York City Department of Buildings announced that it was considering the use of drones to inspect building facades.[21]

Previous innovations are now routine practices in the industry. Lasers have substituted for levels and plumb bobs to establish accurate horizontal and vertical lines. Cordless battery-powered tools have effectively eliminated the hassle of dragging long extension cords through a maze of partially assembled rooms and corridors. Nail guns outpace hammers. Total station is a sophisticated optical instrument used to measure distances and angles. But many of the other inventions breathlessly touted by the industry press remain on the fringes of the industry. Autonomous earth-moving machinery can dig out and prepare foundations. Robots can do layout. Drones can navigate job sites and record daily progress. Exoskeletons can relieve the burden of lifting heavy items, and YouTube videos portray the wonders of 3D printing. Yet many of these advances remain novelty items, available only to a minority of firms that have the resources and inclination to experiment with equipment and systems that have not consistently been proven to be quality or cost-effective.

Despite the cheerleading for disruption and innovation, technology boosters recognize that proclaiming the dawn of a new era may be premature. In a 2020 report, McKinsey & Company futurists predict that 45% of the industry's value chain will shift from traditional processes in the next fifteen years. But even the perpetually optimistic McKinsey consultants recognize the impediments, conceding that only 10 to 12 percent of construction activities will incorporate their lengthy list of recommendations due to "different starting points and abilities to transform."[22] Jeremy Hadall, chief technologist for robotics and automation at the United Kingdom's Manufacturing Technology Centre, adopts a cautionary tone. "People think robots are intelligent. They're getting better, but they're still pretty dumb," he says. "Robots have a place in building productivity in the construction industry," he continues, "but you have to be realistic about what they can do. Are we going to see completely automated robotic building sites in 10 years? No."[23] Similarly, Erin Bradner, Director of Robotics at the Autodesk Robotics Lab, suggests the current level of sophistication of co-bots may be exaggerated: "They'll stop when they encounter an obstacle, but you don't want your project stopping every time a person sneezes."[24] Reza Akhavian, a professor of engineering at San Diego State University, received a $691,000 National Science Foundation grant to study robotics in construction. "Currently and for the foreseeable future, the field of robotics in general, and construction robotics in particular, are not even close to a state in which robots can replace human workers," Akhavian argues. "Robots replacing humans are staples of science fiction movies and cartoons."[25]

There are more fundamental reasons than the irascible and retrograde nature of industry players behind the reluctance to embrace new technology. Robots and other forms of automation are costly and require an extended time frame before presenting a satisfactory return on capital. "There's going to be benefits from some automation, but automation requires investment," notes John Lekfus, president of Rad Technology.[26] Given the decentralized nature of the industry and the predominance of small and medium-sized firms, few owners have the financial capacity to purchase expensive paraphernalia that may only provide a profit in the very long term. There is a structural mismatch between access to resources and hiring control over the personnel to be displaced. Large general contractors may have more cash on hand, but the subcontractors employ the bulk of the workforce. There is little motivation for one well-capitalized company to invest in a technology that will ultimately benefit another smaller firm. Even more important, companies in other industries have traditionally been motivated to spend capital on automation and expensive new procedures to reduce escalating labor costs. Unfortunately, construction executives found a simpler way to cut labor costs through misclassification, cash compensation, and reduced wages and safety standards—all components of a successful crusade to undermine the union sector. There is less incentive to buy robots to replace high-priced labor when the labor itself is no longer pricey. For now, trades workers continue to stuff tape measures, hammers, pliers, utility knives, and other tried-and-true hand tools in their tool belts and carry out their responsibilities in much the same way that their predecessors did.

* * *

In 1910, the French artist Villemard created a series of illustrations imagining life in the year 2000. In one of his drawings, an architect sits in a booth pushing buttons on a console to manipulate a series of machines operating in the context of the usual debris of a construction site. The various machines cut, shape, lift, and place stone blocks to build a house. There are no human laborers in his vision.[27] Contrary to Villemard's concept, machines have not taken over homebuilding but in the last decades of the twentieth century, simple tokens of modernity emerged on construction jobs in the form of fax machines, beepers, and cell phones. Communication between the field and the office and the design professionals improved, allowing for speedier decision making. But the digital revolution in the twenty-first century has propelled construction further, particularly the architectural functions and project management systems. Computer Aided Design (CAD) transformed the design world by utilizing software for architects and engineers to transition from two-dimensional, hand-drawn paper blueprints to three-dimensional computer imaging. The progression of CAD and the widespread dispersion of personal computing into homes and offices in the 1990s allowed tech-savvy contractors to use critical path method scheduling and other sophisticated management systems.

Building Information Modeling (BIM) was the next stage of 3D CAD and has altered the industry in the past fifteen years. BIM introduced the critical factor of coordination into the previously siloed products from the various design disciplines—architectural, structural, mechanical, electrical, civil—and allowed the management team to essentially build a project twice—once virtually on the office desktops and tablets and a second time with the actual trades workers and materials in the field. BIM creates an immersive experience that anticipates and corrects circumstances that are unforeseen by the individual designers. Jeff Gouveia, Executive Vice-President of Suffolk Construction, describes the pre-BIM work style: "Prior to modeling, coordination was done with a light table with a clear piece of plastic over it. You overlaid 2D drawing on top of 2D drawing on top of 2D drawing. You got them just right, taped them in the corner, made sure that they were in the right scale, and then you basically started circling conflicts, where a piece of ductwork or pipe went into a column or a beam."[28] Modeling allows for the advance visualization of an entire development from site-work to finish hardware and the ability to easily incorporate feedback. On renovations, laser scanning can serve a similar purpose by ensuring that the plans correspond precisely to existing dimensions and modeling can then identify possible problems. Surveys of architects, engineers, contractors, and owners overwhelmingly confirm the conclusion that BIM improves the quality and constructability of the final design, accelerates the schedule, and can reduce final costs.[29]

The level of coordination can eliminate the design conflicts that had previously been a chronic source of disputes between contractors, designers, and the affected trades. Modeling shared between project participants provides a "single source of truth." On projects that adopt BIM, buildings are erected more quickly and efficiently, and, presumably, the dynamics between the various actors become more collaborative and less litigious. "The business had become less about building buildings," recalls John Tocci, "and more about arbitration and litigation" over assigning and accepting responsibility for scopes of work. John McLaughlin, president of Sullivan & McLaughlin, a large New England electrical subcontractor, served as a project manager before taking over the family company. He describes his former role at job meetings as "like an attorney getting ready for court. 'I don't own this. I don't own that.'" Now, McLaughlin claims the culture is more collaborative. His company is frequently awarded a project a year before groundbreaking. The intervening time will be spent on regular meetings with all the players to complete the design. "We're all 3D now. We're building that model and we are flying through that on a weekly basis, clash detection, change routing, picking up time and money by shortening distances. We used to get jobs when the steel was up and the building was enclosed and tin [metal studs] was up. Now we are modeling jobs a year in advance."[30]

Modeling likely reduces total construction costs, but it requires upfront investments on a scale that is only available to larger general contractors and a narrow slice of elite subcontractors that can afford the software and, above all, the hiring and training of highly computer-literate staff. John Cannistraro, president of an integrated mechanical subcontracting firm that bids on plumbing, HVAC, and fire protection, describes the challenge. "Let's say it's a huge job, tens of millions of dollars with a requirement for BIM. I may have ten people doing that for a year. So if it was a $20 million subcontract, that's a million bucks to do all that coordination."[31] The investment is an obvious choice for companies like Cannistraro and Sullivan & McLaughlin since each employs hundreds of trades workers and earns well above $100 million in annual revenues, but the practice remains less accessible to smaller firms. Institutional owners like universities and hospitals that expect their projects to last decades are more likely to accept the initial costs of modeling than developers who tend to focus on the bottom line, just surviving through the warranties and short-term flipping goals. Though it is hard to know how representative the sample is, a 2020 technology poll of construction companies reports that only 27% of the firms have BIM departments while 29% do not bother bidding on projects with BIM requirements.[32]

While CAD and BIM initially just involved the professionals, modeling has since filtered down to workers in the field to offer suggestions and critiques of the unfolding designs. BIM meetings often include foremen and lead trades workers. Gouveia describes the transition on a standard task like laying out the sleeves for plumbing and electrical pipes through a concrete deck. "Before, you're unrolling the drawings, the wind is blowing, you've got a piece of rebar on one side, and you've got a brick on the other side, and you're trying to hold it down. Then you're scaling it and going over and using your tape. Now, someone's got a laptop or a tablet or an iPad, with the model on there, with that floor laid out. It's got all the coordinates. You get a stick, walk around, and put the sleeve right there. You laid out that entire deck, and know it's right because it matches the model, and did it in a matter of ninety minutes, whereas before that would have taken maybe five hours. You become a true believer."[33]

McLaughlin has a similar perspective. While some of his long-time foremen were initially reluctant to relinquish methods that had been successful in the past, most have embraced the new approach. He indicates that the feedback is positive as foremen say: "I don't have to worry about the planning, because it was done a year ago. I just print out a copy of what needs to be built, hand it to the journeyman or the apprentice, and say, 'Go, here's your drawing.' Or they can go to an area in the building and they can see it on the screen. I have more time to deal with the emergencies that always pop up because so much of the work has been preplanned."[34] Project information is shared on mobile devices, breaking down barriers between the field and the office. Communication and reporting happen in real time, heading off potential problems.

Though currently limited to larger projects, digitization and modeling will continue to penetrate further into the industry. The 2021 $1.2 trillion Infrastructure Investment and Jobs Act (IIJA) includes $100 million for advanced digital construction management systems and related technologies.[35] While the language in the bill is non-specific, the funds are expected to support advanced digital management tools, 3D modeling, drone visualization, and data analysis. In 2016, the use of BIM was mandated on public projects in the United Kingdom, and the National Institute of Building Sciences (NIBS) hosted a meeting in early 2021 to consider adopting a BIM standard for the United States. Modeling is expanding beyond three dimensions to incorporate 4D (scheduling), 5D (cost), and even 6D (facility management). On the job site, foremen have company-issued tablets as part of their tool kit so plans and modifications can be transmitted instantaneously. The old reliable gang boxes that housed workers' tools for overnight storage now can also have Wi-Fi, printers, and flat screens on the underside of the lid to display the latest shop drawings electronically. Most union training programs have incorporated CAD and BIM into their curricula. New young entrants into the industry from diverse demographic and socio-economic backgrounds may be able to translate their home computer expertise into modeling proficiency in the field. "We are always going to need mechanics to assemble stuff," says John Tocci, "but the mechanic of the future will also be the video game guy."[36]

Factory-produced, pre-fabricated metal wall panels put in place.

7

Building Under a Roof

I n 1926, Walter Gropius, one of the pioneers of modernist architecture, predicted a "fundamental shift of the entire construction business toward industrialization" and went on to insist that "housing will be created no longer at the construction site, but instead at specialized factories with all the ready-to-assemble components," assuring ample capacity and affordability.[1] The allure of building indoors in a controlled environment instead of in the mud, muck, and maelstrom of a conventional site has long motivated some architects, engineers, and construction futurists to promote the virtues of a factory system with assembly lines akin to auto, steel, and other basic industries. Instead of relying on relatively autonomous trades workers moving around a jobsite to carry out complex tasks, industrialized building would be organized around workstations where the components of a finished product would move from worker to worker, whose skills would be more specific and limited but fully coordinated into the larger design. The advantages seemed obvious to Gropius and his supporters. Advanced machinery would churn out standardized identical parts with minute dimensional tolerances, and human error would be eliminated in a well-lit, climate-controlled setting. The completed product would be higher quality and more cost effective, due to scale and non-stop production schedules.

Retailers such as Sears Roebuck and Montgomery Ward implemented aspects of this vision, offering pre-cut mail order homebuilding packages. The Sears kit house was introduced in 1895 and offered to individual buyers through its catalog starting at $700. Ultimately, about half a million were sold until the business faltered in the Great Depression.[2] In the 1930s, thirty-three prefabricated home systems were still on the market.[3] In 1940–41, the federal government initiated a program to build factory housing for defense plant workers. In the first year of the program, 20,000 housing units were produced, but when the war effort wound down and the demand declined, a number of the firms that had been drawn into the program went out of business.[4] The need to rebuild European and Japanese cities damaged during World War II sparked a renewed interested in mass-produced housing abroad. Daiwa House Industry introduced the Pipe House and the Midget House in 1955 and, in a relatively short period of time, prefabricated homes represented over 15% of Japan's new housing stock. In 1964, the Swedish government introduced the *Miljonprogrammet* (Million Homes Program) to build a million new homes in ten years, one-third of which were to be factory-produced, single-family homes.[5]

The industry never took hold in the United States. In 1946, General Panel assumed control of a mothballed Lockheed Aircraft engine plant in Burbank, California, intending to employ 500 workers to build 10,000 houses a year. The approach utilized steel jigs and conveyor belts to generate floor, roof, and ceiling panels in partnership with a distribution dealership arrangement with Celotex Corporation. The venture received widespread publicity but start-up costs proved to be higher than anticipated and, in the absence of the kind of government financial support provided in Europe and Japan, General Panel faltered. Despite a record number of housing starts nationwide, the factory only sold fifteen homes by early 1948. The company was formally dissolved four years later.[6]

In the 1960s, several major corporations, particularly those with a presence in building products, acquired large homebuilders with the intent of introducing modern management techniques and vertical integration. Boise Cascade, for example, was producing 6,000 factory-built homes, 3,000 conventional homes, and 18,000 mobile units by 1968. Even with the introduction of this new breed of corporate managers, 95% of the housing built in that period still used traditional methods.[7] Industrialized building faced too many hurdles. Few private or public investors were prepared to inject the level of funding required to defray the initial capital costs of even the most rudimentarily equipped factories. They worried about the return on investment in the absence of an assurance of widespread demand for the finished product, knowing that most American consumers perceived manufactured homes to be dull, uninspired, cookie-cutter designs.

In May of 1969, U.S. Housing and Urban Development (HUD) Secretary George Romney announced Operation Breakthrough, "a partnership of labor, consumers, private enterprise, local, State and Federal government with the use of modern techniques of production, marketing and management."

Breakthrough had a three-pronged program—design and development, prototype construction, and volume production. In an unusually bold instance of centralized planning for a Republican administration, Breakthrough intended to standardize and industrialize housing parts and modules, leading to the production of twenty-six million homes over a ten-year period. Romney's team negotiated agreements with the Carpenters, Electricians, and Plumbers Unions for both factory-based and on-site work.[8] He hoped to overcome the problem of insufficient demand by providing initial government subsidies and then aggregating a substantial enough market to justify and entice major private capital outlays. At a December news conference, Romney named the thirty-seven finalists out of two hundred thirty-six applicants for Breakthrough funds. Based on the insights of the winning proposals, he said, "factory-built housing was poised to leapfrog over on-site stick-building techniques as the principal method of home construction."[9]

Breakthrough was an unusually activist governmental intervention in a major private market and, as such, drew a high level of interest. *Professional Builder* started a monthly "Industrialized Building" section of its magazine and co-sponsored a 1970 Industrialized Building Congress that attracted over 12,000 attendees. But like previous large-scale forays into industrialized building, Breakthrough ultimately failed. The program ran into a slump in the housing market and federal budget cuts hampered its effectiveness. More fundamentally, the new systems did not realize projected savings. Transportation costs were only viable if the factory was near the ultimate site. Reduced federal funding resulted in diminished subsidies, a crucial factor since the market value of the $126 million prototypes was only $65 million. The program was disbanded in 1973 and Romney was replaced as HUD Secretary. A 1976 General Accounting Office look-back report indicated that only 18,000 units had been built at a cost of $72 million and concluded that Breakthrough had not led to major changes in the housing industry. The report determined that "conventional building is cheaper."[10]

Ironically, as the dream of a vibrant, high-quality industrial home withered, a low-cost variant survived without any public subsidies or fawning publicity. A 1970 article in *Progressive Architecture* reported that the mobile home industry was thriving just as Romney's scheme was struggling. "In effect," the authors wrote, "the mobile home manufacturers created their own Breakthrough without an operation."[11] Mobile homes have always had their own discreet economic structure. Fabricated in factories, they were distributed through a system similar to auto sales. Thousands of retail dealers sold individual mobile homes, provided financing options, and often operated the trailer parks where the mobile homes were to be located. The homeowner bought the unit and then paid monthly fees to lease the land and water and electrical infrastructure. This low-cost path to homeownership emerged as a small but stable piece of the U.S. housing puzzle, particularly in rural communities. Mobile homes constituted roughly one-quarter of all new single-family dwellings in the late 1970s. Half were located in trailer parks where they were functionally immobile homes. A far cry from Gropius's plea for an aesthetically attractive manufactured home, the 14' × 70' single wides were cheap, functional, and unassuming. A 1978 study listed perception barriers to widespread acceptance including their small size, low quality materials and workmanship, location in unacceptable neighborhoods, and even the very name "mobile home."[12]

* * *

Digital technologies spawned another variation of industrialized building. Millworking and sheet metal shops introduced Computer Numerical Control (CNC) processes into their equipment, allowing computers to guide the cutting and shaping of metal and wood without the regular ministrations of a manual operator. CNC is a high precision subtractive procedure in which a computer program directs drills, mills, lathes, and other tools to chip away at a workpiece until the desired product is formed—a refined and mechanized variant of a sculptor chiseling a design from an inanimate block of stone. The operator programs the computer and launches the activity while the machine does all the actual work. The subsequent advent of CAD and BIM prompted renewed eruptions of enthusiasm for twenty-first-century factory production. The combination of sophisticated software and accurate machinery in the context of a controlled environment promised to usher in a golden era of advanced building technology unimaginable to its early advocates.

The cheerleading was fast and furious. A 2011 McGraw-Hill Construction report declared "This is not your grandpa's prefab!" and confidently claimed that significant productivity gains were available due to BIM's contributions and the enhanced quality provided by modern materials and manufacturing facilities.[13] A few years later, architect, technologist, and educator Phil Bernstein wrote an article on the future of construction titled "Your Next Building Won't Be Built—It Will Be Manufactured." According to Bernstein, the mass-manufactured building industry had reached maturity and was on the cusp of defining a new paradigm. He advised, "Check the trailer-park stereotype at the door."[14] The McGraw-Hill report had surveyed 800 contractors, architects, and engineers. Over forty percent of the respondents stated that they were using some form of off-site production on healthcare facilities, college dormitories, and manufacturing plants. These types of structures—along with hotels and multiunit apartments—lent themselves to an assembly line orientation because they had repetitive design concepts. Every dorm room, every hotel room, every apartment could be identical and offered economies of scale based on consistent software programming and the constant repetition of tasks on the shop floor.

Mark Skender, CEO of Skender, a Chicago-based design and construction firm, argued that modularization would become much more common as more people understood the potential for "industry disruption." At the 2019 opening of its offshoot Skender Manufacturing, the company's chief technology officer mocked the "Stone Age methods" of on-site construction. With the debut of the new plant, he proclaimed, "we're completely changing the paradigm for the construction process."[15] Nick Campisano, CEO of a real estate and venture capital firm, doubled down on the parade, declaring that modular construction would "trend towards nearly 100 percent market share of all large commercial projects. It is," he said, "without a doubt, the way of the future."[16]

There are a variety of off-site factory building products, ranging in complexity from the prefabrication of individual components, such as pre-hung window and door frames, to panelized wall and floor systems, to full-scale modular, or volumetric, rectangular finished boxes. The interiors of these boxes are steel or wood-framed, sheetrocked, wired, plumbed, and painted, and can include fixtures and appliances. Once outside the doors of the factory, they are trucked to the site, hoisted in place by a crane, connected to outside utilities and to each other, and, after exterior finishes are applied, are ready for occupancy. The assembly is virtually plug and play. The appeal of the full modular system is understandable. The architectural design is coordinated with factory engineers and technicians, every individual element in the plans is digitized, pieces are machine pre-cut and fitted to exact dimensions, subassemblies are moved from station to station by conveyor or overhead crane, and the entire process takes place in a comfortable setting free from Mother Nature's whims.

A study conducted for the Modular Building Institute (MBI), the industry's primary trade association, suggested that these advantages would create a 16% savings in total costs and a 45% schedule compression compared to conventional construction.[17] As long as there are no unexpected delays, the projection of a shorter schedule has proven to be accurate. Assuming the drawings are detailed and complete, the factory can begin production of the volumetric boxes while on-site subcontractors are excavating and erecting foundation walls. As soon as the foundation and mechanical systems are in place, the boxes can be set in place and the connecting crews can close in the building. The simultaneous activities at two separate locations dramatically reduce the project's expected completion date. Instead of the traditional sequencing of foundations, framing, mechanical systems, interior finishes, and exterior finishes—one after the other—the framing and finishes can be completed in the factory while or even before the hole is dug and the concrete is poured. From a developer's perspective, the expedited timeline can be a financial bonanza, saving months of carrying and overhead costs. The charges for site management, material handling, and project management as well as the interest paid on construction loans can be cut in half if the project goes smoothly. Furthermore, the finished development can be brought to market faster, allowing hotel rooms to have "heads on beds" and apartments to be leased more quickly, thereby jumpstarting the flow of revenue.

A new lexicon has emerged from the emphasis on more offsite component manufacturing. Advocates call for a paradigm shift from project-centric to product-centric and from build-to-order (BTO) to engineer-to-order (ETO). The reimagined jargon and the presumed benefits have prompted celebrity investors like Warren Buffett to target modular construction. Berkshire Hathaway's MiTek engineered building products and construction software firm has launched a hybrid offsite-onsite building model aimed at hospitality, health care, education, and multifamily construction.[18] And the high-tech world has taken notice of the chatter about the industry leaving its antiquated ways behind. In early 2021, Gonzalo Gonzalez left Tesla to join New York City-based modular developer iBUILT as its chief manufacturing officer. iBUILT launched in November 2020 and within a little over a year had negotiated $1 billion in new deals. Explaining his choice to leave the cutting-edge electric vehicle company for a modular firm, Gonzalez uttered the overused term: "iBUILT is disruptive."[19]

The hopeful projections and rosy scenarios have not always panned out. The expense of producing boxes is still only approximately half of total project costs. The excavation, foundation, trucking, crane operation, and buttoning up the modules are all on the on-site side of the ledger, limiting the overall impact of potential savings from factory production. Transportation can be a budget killer. Depending on the region, it may not be worthwhile to haul modules further than one hundred miles. Financing also remains a major challenge. Though the carrying costs may be reduced due to the expedited schedule, most construction lenders will not release any draws on the loans until the first batch of modules arrives on the site, placing all the burden of up-front costs on the manufacturer. As a result, factory managers will frequently ask for as much as fifty percent of the total budget in advance to cover procurement and production, a request that most owner/developers consider excessive. Beyond the inherent boom-and-bust cycles of the industry, the primary cause of modular factory closure is inadequate cash flow and under-capitalization.

While the bottom line on individual projects varies widely, the modular industry has not demonstrated that it can consistently build projects more cheaply. The factory-based workforce is paid far less than its outside counterparts, but that significant gap has not always been enough to produce surpluses for development teams. Even the McKinsey evangelists sounded a cautionary note. A 2019 study claimed that modules could deliver 20%-50% schedule compression and have the "potential" to yield significant costs savings, but "that is still more the exception than the norm." In what was otherwise an enthusiastic paean to the virtues of modular, the report noted that there is an opportunity for 20% cost savings but a real risk of the very opposite—that is, up to a 10% increase in costs "if labor savings are outweighed by logistics or material costs."[20]

For all of the commotion about the marvels of modular, there are enough problematic high-profile real-world examples to support McKinsey's unexpected caution. In 2015, the Marriott hotel chain decided to build its new signature hotels on a modular basis. Marriott hired architect, television host and modular proselytizer Danny Forster to design the world's tallest modular hotel on 6th Avenue in Manhattan. Forster's firm's website shows a team of black-clad professionals gazing at the camera under the motto: "we value the challenge of innovation over the security of repetition."[21] The hotel's guest rooms were built in a Polish factory and shipped in 2019 to a Brooklyn dock where they remain under waterproof membranes. Signage on the Sixth Avenue site proclaimed a March 2020 anticipated completion date. Over two and a half years later (as of this writing) the project is still dormant, consisting of partially completed foundations, perhaps due to the pandemic-induced downturn in the hospitality industry or perhaps because of a dozen or more liens filed by subcontractors for unpaid bills.[22] Like other New York projects, the Marriott project would have had to contend with the challenges of trying to operate in a dense urban environment. The boxes must cross older bridges and be driven through narrow streets filled with traffic, limiting their potential size. Once at the destination, they have to be set in place immediately since there is no room for storage, and the types of cranes required to lift the load to multistory heights can be cost prohibitive. In this particular case, an enormously valuable piece of real estate in midtown Manhattan continues to be little more than a hole in the ground.

Forest City's CEO Bruce Ratner promised to solve these kinds of problems with the ambitious $6 billion Atlantic Yards development in Brooklyn launched in 2012. The original goal was to erect fifteen modular buildings, some as high as fifty stories. Ratner told skeptics that he had "cracked the code." Atlantic Yards would save time and money and combine greater affordability and more sustainability in the context of world-class architecture. The work was to be carried out in warehouses at the Brooklyn Navy Yard in a partnership with global construction manager Skanska. Sixty percent of the total project would be built in the factory and trucked to the Prospect Heights neighborhood in Brooklyn for completion.[23] One of the first projects, a 363-unit tower flanking the Barclays Center, suffered from leaks, incomplete modules, cost overruns, and lengthy delays before finally opening in 2016. Skanska blamed Forest City for an inadequate design and Forest City fired back, charging Skanska with poor execution. Forest City bought out Skanska's interest and then sold the development to Chinese government-owned Greenland USA, which rebranded the project as Pacific Park. In 2018, the former partners reached a confidential settlement of three costly and bitter lawsuits involving tens of millions of dollars plus damages. Bruce Ratner abandoned Forest City for the world of philanthropy.[24]

Silicon Valley had been watching the growing embrace of technology in the world of construction. Tech executives like Michael Marks proposed bringing transformative business strategies to the building process. Marks had been the CEO of Flextronics, an electronics manufacturing company, and, along with partner Fritz Wolff, unveiled Katerra in 2015. Katerra's business proposition consisted of handling all aspects of the building process, responsible for financing, property acquisition, architectural design, software engineering, materials procurement, factory-based construction, and even the ultimate management of a building. The company would buy materials and fixtures like sinks and faucets in bulk, skipping the middlemen and selling directly to general contractors. If the general contractors hesitated to use the designated products, Katerra would step in to assume the contracting role. Katerra's holistic and seemingly revolutionary vision was welcomed by the tech community, in particular the hallowed Japanese venture investment firm SoftBank. SoftBank's funds and imprimatur allowed Katerra to reach a $1 billion valuation by April of 2017. Marks and his team used the money on a spending spree, acquiring eighteen companies including six architecture and contracting groups. Katerra and its subsidiaries established a vertically integrated supply chain that manufactured virtually every element of a building from modules to lightbulbs.[25]

In January 2018, SoftBank's Vision Fund led a new $865 million round of financing followed by another $700 million a year later. Having grown to a $4 billion valuation, Katerra had raised money faster than it could deliver product on the street. The company struck deals before having figured out how to mass-produce parts and make the model work. Architects designed projects dependent on Katerra parts, only to learn the links on the supply chain had not yet been forged. Contracts were signed based on unrealistic projections, and the business development group would only then turn to in-house estimators to generate actual cost estimates. A former estimator suggested there were frequently gaps of millions of dollars. An internal investigation later determined that company financial statements had been "intentionally misstated."[26]

Marks impatiently blamed the difficulties on Covid and the traditional industry's slow-moving mindset and unwillingness to recognize and accept the value of disruption. Nonetheless, co-founder Wolff left in November 2019 amid layoffs and abandoned projects. In December, Katerra shut down its Phoenix modular building plant, laid off two hundred workers, and relocated to a more highly automated facility in Tracy, California, with lower labor costs. The firm continued to promote its brand aggressively, signing a $650 million contract with Saudi Arabia in January 2020 to build 8,000 homes, but internal troubles continued to mount. Despite the infusion of SoftBank cash, the company was running out of money. Marks's solution was to go even bigger and add the developer role to the company's vertical integration in order to increase profits. But the helter skelter acquisition approach of constant expansion with new in-house subsidiaries and external partners prevented adequate vetting. In February 2020, the New Jersey Department of Labor issued a stop work order and assessed penalties on a subcontractor on a Jersey City Katerra project for misclassification and cash compensation of its workers.[27]

In May, Marks was pushed out. Additional layoffs followed in June and Katerra filed in bankruptcy court a year later. The Tracy plant was sold in August 2021 for a fire sale price of $21.5 million to Volumetric Building Companies, whose CEO termed Katerra's failure "spectacular." After four senior staff members landed jobs with Modulous, a construction technology firm in London, CEO Chris Bone said politely, "We're looking to achieve the same as Katerra . . . from a completely different angle." In its 2019 report on modular construction, McKinsey had named Katerra and Skender as two of the leading examples of the exciting embrace of an "integrated technology platform across the construction value chain" that included architectural design, engineering fabrication, materials production, and construction. The authors viewed SoftBank's ongoing financial commitment as the tech world's seal of approval and a "promising sign . . . of staying power." A year after that report, Skender Manufacturing closed its doors and two years later, Katerra filed for bankruptcy protection.[28]

Despite the high-flying crashes, the modular sector of the industry has maintained a presence, accounting for 5.5% of new construction in 2021 in North America, according to the Modular Building Institute (MBI). Still, the higher expectations have not been met. "Everyone needs to stop and unlearn what they know about building and relearn how this modular stuff has to be sequenced, staged, orchestrated and coordinated with all the infrastructure," said Jared Bradley, president of a Nashville, Tennessee-based architecture firm.[29] The companies that appear to be stable and successful are those with construction experience and a sharper focus that is less susceptible to the call of the disruptive siren. Todd Benson took Bensonwood Homes from a niche timber framing company in the 1970s to a manufacturing facility in southern New Hampshire that turns out about three hundred high-end energy efficient homes a year. Benson invested $13 million to build and fit out his state-of-the-art plant with German and Canadian milling and nailing machines and was able to achieve a positive revenue flow within six months. Many of the workers are CAD proficient and carry out their duties on the shop floor with a tool cart that has a laptop in the top tray and chisels, planes, and other hand tools in the lower trays.[30]

Larry Pace is the principal in Cannon Constructors. a well-established general contracting firm in the Bay Area that has focused on multiunit residential construction since the 1980s. In 2014, his real estate development partner Rick Holliday suggested they consider a modular project. "I wasn't real enthusiastic about it," remembers Pace. "I'd heard all the war stories and failures and went into it kicking and screaming." They raised $22 million and took over the 258,000 square foot Building 680, a former machine shop on the decommissioned Mare Island naval shipyard in Vallejo. The building was ideal for their purposes as was Vallejo, a blue-collar community with a sizable worker pool. Pace and Holliday plotted their future with an additional partner, the Northern California Regional Council of Carpenters. Cannon had always been a union company and, as Pace put it, "it was an absolute no brainer" to start the new venture as a unionized plant. Jay Bradshaw, head of the union, agreed: "We try to stay ahead of new technologies coming online. Not fight it, but support it, train for it, and organize it." Bradshaw helped Pace and Holliday identify the Mare Island location and the union recruited and trained much of the workforce.[31]

FactoryOS has been a success. With the housing shortage in the Bay Area, their products—boxes with completely finished interiors—are in high demand. There are about five hundred workers in both Building 680 and a second building that opened in the shipyard, turning out 1,500 units a year. Another plant is planned for Southern California. Pace has become a convert.

He insists the FactoryOS product is 20% cheaper, can be built 40% faster, and can achieve architectural detail and variety on the buildings' exteriors. The workers operate under an industrial collective bargaining agreement, earning roughly half of an outside union carpenter's hourly wage along with health coverage, but the work is steady and overtime is plentiful. FactoryOS has earned a reputation as a welcoming second chance employer for workers with no or minimal construction experience. Franklin Carroll is a framing lead in the factory. "I grew up in foster care, went to jail at 25," says Carroll. Unskilled when hired, he started sheetrocking, moved to framing, and now trains others. "I have a computer screen with a touchscreen, moveable 47 inch monitor, and get plans in my phone through BIM 360 . . . FactoryOS helped me save my life," he concludes.[32]

The controversy over modular will continue, but there is no disputing that off-site production has been and will be increasing, particularly in the form of prefabrication. Years ago, carpenters would install a door by building a frame, mortising the hinges, hanging the door to make sure it was plumb and level, boring holes for the doorknob, setting the hardware, and trimming out the unit on both sides. Today in standard on-site construction, the framers simply leave a dimensioned opening, and a pre-hung door with pre-bored hardware holes arrives on the job to be set in place. Window installation has followed the same track. Trades workers have long travelled a slow but steady path from highly skilled fabricators to installers of factory-made products they once crafted by hand. Specialization has added to the deskilling trajectory. Some electricians do power and lighting, others do teledata. Some carpenters do concrete foundations, some do framing and sheetrock, some install ceilings or flooring, and others do finish work. There remains crossover and a role for the generalist, particularly in renovation, maintenance, and service work, but contractors' desire for speed, efficiency, and enhanced production on new projects encourages subdivisions within trades.

There are multiple examples of effective hybrids—that is, factory-style methods that do not depend on a highly capitalized permanent plant. A panelizing shop requires minimal investment and can be shut down if a particular project is not at the stage when the need for wall, roof, or floor panels is urgent. Workers can be moved from the site to the shop to take advantage of weather-free conditions and return to the site for installation. There are even creative examples of bringing the factory to the site, as in the case of an eighteen-story residential building in London that moved a "jump factory" from floor to floor with gantry cranes, completing the work in eighteen weeks without an accident and a 75% reduction of on-site material waste.[33] Still, that ambitious project was well over budget and required the kind of initial investment possible for only a small fraction of the global contracting community.

Amy Marks, the self-styled "Queen of Prefab," argues that construction employers must shift their mindset from being contractors to becoming manufacturers,[34] but most general contractors today conceive of off-site work as an evolutionary shift that is incorporated into an existing orientation. Jim Grossman, founder of Rise Construction, acknowledges that volumetric finished boxes may have a role but suggests they are inherently limited to projects based on repetitive design elements. He argues that panelized walls, bathrooms, and other components are more widely used. "People are doing [modules]," says Grossman, "but somebody standing up a panelized product, that's where I think today's world is."[35]

John Cannistraro has set up a permanent panelization shop in the Seaport district of Boston. His company directly employs the pipe trades—plumbers, pipefitters, and sprinklerfitters—as well as sheet metal workers, and he can bring in carpenters and electricians through other local subcontracting firms. The work situation is ideal for complex components like hospital head walls behind a patient's bed that have an unusual level of built-in mechanical elements. The carpenters frame the stud walls, the plumbers pipe all the medical gas lines, the electricians install the wiring, the assembled walls are shrink wrapped, shipped to the job, and hoisted to their location. "We've doubled the amount of off-site fabrication we do in the last ten years," says Cannistraro, "and it will double again in the next five or ten years."[36] John McLaughlin of Sullivan & McLaughlin has adopted a similar model, albeit less extensive. He is unconvinced about full-scale modular construction but recognizes the advantages of, for example, building the electrical rooms for a project in advance. But he points out that those cases require the kind of forward planning that is still limited to larger projects with knowledgeable owners and general contractors. "I'm going to do it three or even six months in advance, so there can't be any changes," he cautions. "It's a ton of extra steps, but the quality is much better." Prefabrication works, he continues, because of the coordination that BIM and 3D modeling offers.

From a worker's perspective, the reality of off-site production may not be new, but its use is escalating. It is part of a gradual long-term deskilling trend of specialization and the shift from fabricator to installer. Semi-skilled jobs in a factory certainly offer less opportunity for autonomy and creativity and provide lower compensation, even at unionized plants, than on-site construction work. Off-site work of the kind that Cannistraro and Sullivan & McLaughlin perform maintains more continuity. Their union trades workers perform similar tasks whether on the site or in the shop and receive the same wages and benefits. For all the clamor about disruption and innovation, transformative business models have experienced as much failure as success and are, in any case, restricted to a small segment of the industry. For the most part, construction workers continue to put on their boots, hard hats, and tool belts every day and operate along familiar lines. Rise's Grossman, who prides himself on thinking about the industry's future, concludes, "I cannot come across a scenario where we really pull the workforce out of what's happening in the field."[37]

Tool belt with assortment of hand tools.

8

Many Rivers to Cross: Organizing and Diversity

The building trades unions have often been described as the principal oc-
cupants of the conservative wing of the House of Labor. Brief sketches
of three top leaders from the past reflect that assessment. William "Big Bill"
Hutcheson became president of the United Brotherhood of Carpenters and
Joiners of America in 1915. A conservative Republican, he was a vocal op-
ponent of the New Deal and any federal legislation aimed at softening the
impact of the Great Depression. Perhaps his most famous moment came in
1935, when he was on the receiving end of John L. Lewis's "punch heard 'round
the world" in an AFL convention altercation over the issue of industrial
unionism. During a raucous debate marred by bickering over parliamentary
procedures, Lewis, the fiery head of the United Mine Workers, challenged
Hutcheson and other labor chieftains to support the importance of organizing workers across all occupations and industries. In the face of the AFL's
unyielding allegiance to a more exclusive craft model of trade unionism,
Lewis and his allies walked out and later formed the independent Congress
of Industrial Organizations (CIO), sparking the greatest mass mobilization
of workers in the nation's history. Hutcheson never modified his views. After
thirty-seven years as head of the Carpenters Union, he retired in 1952, turning over the reins to his son Maurice.

George Meany was the son of a union plumber who followed in his father's
footsteps. He became a business agent for New York's Local 463 in 1922 and
gradually worked his way up the labor hierarchy, as an officer in the city's
Building Trades Council and then president of the New York State AFL.
Meany assumed the presidency of the national AFL in 1952 and set out to
bring the CIO back into the federation. After lengthy and, at times, difficult

negotiations, Meany effectuated a merger in 1955 and served as president of the newly formed AFL-CIO until his retirement in 1979. A gruff, cigar-smoking, blunt-spoken man, he comfortably fit the stereotype of an American labor leader of the era.

Though Meany served as the principal voice for the nation's labor movement for more than two decades, his formative years in the building trades heavily influenced his underlying union philosophy. He proudly claimed he had never led a strike nor walked a picket line because the contractors who employed his union's members never sought to replace their skilled workforce. In 1972, a reporter asked Meany why union membership was not growing as fast as the nation's labor force. Meany responded: "I don't know, I don't care." He turned on the interviewer and asked why he should "worry about organizing groups of people who do not want to be organized." Meany went on, "I used to worry about the size of the membership. But quite a few years ago I just stopped worrying about it, because to me it doesn't make any difference."[1]

Peter Brennan, son of a New York union ironworker, joined the Painters Union as a young man and was elected as business manager of his local in 1947. Ten years later, he became president of the New York Building and Construction Trades Council. Brennan emerged as a national figure when he vehemently opposed Mayor John Lindsay's 1968 Executive Order to increase minority participation in the city's construction industry. Challenges to racial exclusion in construction were mounting in northern cites as part of the burgeoning civil rights movement. The Nixon administration had tentatively supported the Philadelphia Plan, a program that established hiring goals for nonwhite workers on federal construction contracts. Lindsay, a Kennedy-esque moderate Republican, proposed a New York affirmative action plan with the backing of Nixon's Labor Department. However, sympathy for the growing anti-Vietnam War movement, particularly in the wake of the May 4, 1970 shooting of four students at Kent State University, transformed the political priorities of the Nixon White House. Brennan organized two rallies in May in support of Nixon's Southeast Asian policies that came to be known as the "Hard Hat Riots," as pro-war construction workers attacked and beat anti-war protesters in the streets of lower Manhattan.

Charles Colson, advisor to Nixon and later one of the Watergate Seven, quickly invited a delegation of twenty-two labor leaders including Brennan to the White House on May 26. Colson's gesture was a piece of the administration's "emerging Republican majority" strategy to wean organized labor off its attachment to the Democratic Party by highlighting a perception of declining working class worth emanating from the urban cultural elitists who were presumably the new Democratic power brokers. In the run-up to the 1972 presidential election, AFL-CIO leaders were concerned that their influence was waning with the candidacy of Senator George McGovern. Nixon's team worked quietly to eliminate the usual anti-labor planks in their party's platform and aggressively wooed national union leaders. The courtship was effective. In the end, Meany bucked the tradition of labor endorsements of Democratic candidates and stayed neutral in the race. In that year's electoral landslide, Nixon received 57% of the manual worker vote and 54% of the union vote.[2]

Brennan had used the occasion of the White House meeting to lobby for a severely watered-down version of Lindsay's New York Plan. In exchange, he offered to go one step further than Meany, and publicly endorsed Nixon for president. Under pressure, Lindsay backed off his earlier hiring objectives and Brennan was rewarded with an appointment as Secretary of Labor in the new Cabinet. Meany initially applauded the nomination but ultimately broke with Brennan over the administration's meager minimum wage guidelines. In Brennan's *New York Times* obituary, Republican Congressman Peter King recalled that "more than any other individual, [Brennan] was responsible for bringing the blue-collar labor Democrats" into the Republican fold.[3]

Hutcheson, Meany, and Brennan may be remembered for their stances on broad national political issues, but their orientation set the tone for and mirrored the views of most building trades labor leaders on the ground. Their style of business unionism—emphasizing limiting the pool of skilled workers in order to maintain control of local labor markets—was embedded in the culture of building trades unions from top to bottom. Thousands of local unions dotted the country's landscape and the constitutional structure of the national unions fostered decentralization and granted substantial autonomy and authority to local officers in each of the trades. Interventions by the Washington, DC-based Internationals were rare. Local business agents frequently had stronger day-to-day ties with construction employers in their geographical jurisdiction than with leaders in the upper echelons of their own union or, for that matter, other labor officials in their communities. Meany's disdain for organizing was broadly shared. It was seen as an irrelevant activity made unnecessary by decades of strong market share, access to the sole skilled labor pool, and a consequent presumption of permanent union strength.

A cautious and conservative stance was both rational and understandable since it had apparently worked for years. The role of business agents was largely limited to supplying manpower to contractors on an as-needed basis and administering the training and benefit programs. Organizing consisted of an occasional conversation with a new employer entrant into the industry. Tales of corruption inevitably arose in situations where unions tightly controlled local markets, but the reality was that a business unionist orientation was as much of an obstacle to growth and transformation as dishonesty. Members wanted to be serviced and, similar to participants in many professional organizations, preferred that a lid be kept on membership levels to maximize employment opportunities.

As union strength in construction began to decline, complacency, inaction, and a reliance on behind-the-scenes political relationships were no longer enough. A younger generation of leaders questioned the passive attitudes of their predecessors as they watched the influence of their unions inexorably slipping away while the non-union sector gathered steam. Some local unions added organizers to their staff but, without a tradition of strategic organizing practices, these new roles were not clearly defined and they largely functioned as business agents-in-waiting. In the early 1990s, a program called COMET (Construction Organizing Membership Education Training) was launched with the endorsement of all fifteen general presidents of the unions affiliated with the national Building & Construction Trades Department (BCTD). COMET was a three-hour educational program aimed at persuading rank-and-file members to reverse their unions' long-standing allergy to organizing. In a clear rebuke of the Meany worldview, BCTD President Robert Georgine flatly stated that the unions should not rest "unless and until every construction worker belongs to a union. Universal membership is our goal."[4]

COMET trainers understood that the conventional wisdom among both officers and members was the opposite, that is, that expanding their ranks by recruiting the unorganized meant union members would have to compete with these newly organized workers for a fixed or even shrinking number of jobs. Developed by a team led by Jeff Grabelsky of the Cornell Industrial and Labor Relations School and a union electrician, the COMET training consisted of a series of sobering graphs demonstrating shrinking union market share, declining industry wage and benefit levels, and the futility of concessionary bargaining. Union give-backs had only succeeded in setting off a "race to the bottom" in which compensation was dwindling for both union and non-union workers. A series of participatory exercises sought to break down assumptions about union viability and the competency of non-union trades workers. In the context of diminishing union density, maintaining barriers to entry was counterproductive and a recipe for future irrelevance. For union members who had come out of the non-union sector, the material resonated with their work histories; for members who had entered the union apprenticeship programs directly and only worked under the protection of a collective bargaining agreement, much of the content of COMET was eye-opening and revelatory.

Within a few years, tens of thousands of union trades workers had gone through the training. COMET pins, stickers, and t-shirts were common on job sites around the country. A follow-up survey of union officials indicated before-and-after swings in perceptions resulting in a heightened acceptance of outreach to non-union workers. The wide dispersal of the program and the enthusiasm that it engendered set off alarm bells among non-union employers. In a 1993 letter to his members, the ABC's president warned: "Don't think that COMET is another 'flash-in-the-pan' effort . . . The success or failure of your business is directly related to ABC's ability to 'shoot down COMET.'"[5] The ABC letter may have been an effective fundraising tool, but the panic was excessive and overwrought. Business unionism had been too deeply entrenched for too long. The creation and implementation of the COMET program reflected a realization that union strategies needed to be re-invented, and its analysis offered a thoughtful understanding of what had occurred. It was an educational program that effectively challenged hide-bound beliefs. Georgine's words may have been stirring and a useful corrective, and COMET may have kickstarted necessary discussions about organizing, but neither offered a comprehensive plan to re-establish union primacy and elevate conditions in the industry.

Opening the doors to the unions also required a reckoning with the history of racial barriers that haunted the industry. African Americans had been systematically excluded from union ranks. In those few cases where craftsmen had become union members, it was often as part of a segregated local. An Oakland plumber's experience was more typical. When he tried to join Local 445 in 1945, "I was told that the union could not put me to work because most of the people (white) requesting plumbing work done in their home definitely did not want a Negro plumber." He traveled the only path available, taking the state licensing examination to go into business for himself.[6] Matters had not improved two decades later. The numbers varied slightly from region to region, and the basic trades tended to be somewhat less restrictive than the licensed mechanical trades. But even in cities with large minority populations, the presence on jobsites was miniscule. A federal administrator reported that in Chicago, Blacks represented 3.8% of the city's union electricians, 0.7% of the carpenters, and 0.1% of sheet metal workers.[7] In New York City, 92% of building trades union members were white, including every single one of the 3,300 members of Sheet Metal Workers Local 28.[8]

With the high visibility of white construction workers on urban sites serving as a constant reminder of lack of access, protests became commonplace starting in the early 1960s. Organizations sprang up in Philadelphia, Chicago, Detroit, Brooklyn, Newark, San Francisco, Boston, and other cities to pressure the industry to desegregate. The federal government initially endorsed the Philadelphia Plan's objectives as a model but, in every city, contractors and unions alike opposed implementation. In some cases, the opposition was virulent. In September 1969, Undersecretary of Labor Arthur Fletcher scheduled a hearing at a hotel in Chicago to propose extending the Philadelphia Plan principles. Thirty-five hundred white workers filled the meeting room and spilled over to demonstrate outside. After twenty minutes of verbal abuse and fearful complaints from the hotel management, Fletcher was forced to recess the session.[9]

Catholic social activist John Cort attributed the hostility to a "nightmarish memory" of the massive unemployment of the Great Depression handed down in tales from father to son. "There is racial discrimination," Cort testified to the U. S. Commission on Civil Rights, but in addition, workers "operate on the theory that as long as there is any union member who is or might be unemployed, they are not going to admit additional union members."[10] Cort's comments minimized the extent of open racism, but the combination of racial animus and an insular mentality had produced near-universal initial opposition to expanding minority participation—as much or more so from the employer community as the unions.

The cumulative impact of continued protests gradually eased barriers. In some cities, community activists shifted tactics to endorse broad residency objectives rather than goals limited to racial participation, calculating that an alliance between urban white and Black workers might be more politically palatable. Chuck Turner, a leader of the Third World Workers' Association, re-formed his organization as the Boston Jobs Coalition. Looking back, Turner commented: "We saw the only thing that would save affirmative action in the trades was an alliance with white Boston residents." In 1979, Mayor Kevin White signed an executive order implementing the Coalition's program—50% of the jobs to residents, 25% to minorities, and 10% to women—on city-funded and large private projects. The order was codified as an ordinance four years later.[11]

In 1988, the ABC and its allies put a measure on the November ballot to repeal the Massachusetts prevailing wage law. Initial polling indicated a strong preference to support the initiative. The state's labor movement mobilized in an unprecedented fashion, developing a powerful grass-roots movement. The Vote No campaign recognized that it would have to build support beyond the building trades even though Question 2's impact was limited to publicly funded construction projects. By re-framing the issue as one of corporate greed and people vs. profits, the messaging resonated with a majority of voters. The creation of a coalition that included civil rights organizations and community groups revealed the building trades' increased willingness—born of necessity—to broaden horizons and redefine priorities. Historical resentments had to be overcome to generate endorsements. Ultimately, the proposed repeal was defeated by a 58–42 margin with wealthier suburban communities voting in favor and working-class neighborhoods voting in opposition. Boston's four predominantly Black wards voted down Question 2 by an overwhelming 4–1 edge, a striking outcome given the background of racial conflict.[12]

The scrutiny of the union sector of construction has had a salutary effect. The harsh light focused on the troubling history forced unionized contractors and unions to respond—at first with hostility and then, with modest reforms. Non-union employers, however, were under no similar compunction and have continued to reflect problematic historical patterns. A 2013 study in New York City showed an ongoing overall underrepresentation in construction, as Black workers comprised 16.5% of the construction workforce compared to 23.3% of all employed workers. The study also revealed a union-non-union divide. Blacks held 21.3% of the city's union jobs, but only 13.8% of the non-union jobs.[13] Black union construction workers in New York City earn 36.1% more than Black nonunion construction workers, a reminder of the advantages of working under a collective bargaining agreement.

In an era of mounting white supremacist activity, reports of nooses placed on nearly twenty construction sites have surfaced since the murder of George Floyd in May 2020. Racist graffiti shut down the sprawling $1 billion Meta (formerly Facebook) data center jobsite in Eagle Mountain, Utah, on three separate occasions,[14] and the 3.6 million-sq. ft. Amazon warehouse in Windsor, Connecticut, was closed twice after eight ropes tied as nooses were found.[15] There was widespread condemnation of these incidents from local community leaders but, since both were non-union projects, there were no worker representatives to speak out or take action. No one has been apprehended. Sadly, this form of racist behavior remains far too widespread and has crossed into union territory. A noose was discovered on another Meta site with a union workforce in Redmond, Washington, in 2022. Ultimately, three workers were held accountable and fired. When a similar event occurred on a project near Oakridge, Tennessee, the North America's Building Trades Unions (NABTU) quickly condemned "such hateful and racist acts" and expressed a zero tolerance policy. NABTU set up a hotline and offered a $200,000 reward for information about the parties involved. Within a few weeks, the responsible individual was identified based on tips to the hotline, and immediately fired.[16] Individual union members may engage in hateful actions, but their organizations are increasingly prepared to denounce the behavior and support sanctions.

The issue of race remains a defining political factor in our society and, most certainly, within the construction industry. While the overall situation has improved, there is no shortage of continuing covert and overt instances of racial animosity. Activists contend that many of the programs in place are still inadequate.[17] Progress has varied from city to city and trade to trade, but the trend lines on union jobs are more promising. Many communities now have pre-apprenticeship programs that serve as a pipeline for people of color and women to be introduced to the trades and enter union apprenticeships. The best lens to forecast the demographics of the future workforce is a review of apprenticeship numbers. In a study of employment patterns at California's renewable energy power plants, the share of people of color entering apprenticeship programs in the three major trades reached 60% in 2017.[18] The percentage of African Americans among registered union apprentices in New York City doubled from 1994 to 2014.[19] In 2010, the New York State Department of Labor reported that 63% of union apprentices were minorities.[20] In 2011, Leah Rambo, an African American tradeswoman, was appointed Director of Training for Sheet Metal Workers Local 28, the local that did not have a single Black member forty years earlier.

In 1950, men constituted 97% of all construction employment.[21] Since those numbers included secretaries, receptionists, bookkeepers, and other traditionally female roles in construction company offices, it is reasonable to assume that the presence of tradeswomen in the field was virtually nonexistent. In 1978, President Jimmy Carter issued an executive order setting goals and timetables for the hiring and training of women on federally funded construction contracts, triggering the emergence of a group of pioneering tradeswomen around the country. Confronted with resistance ranging from aggressive hostility and harassment to patronizing ridicule, women struggled to remain on the job. Even some of the sympathetic male colleagues expected the newcomers to act with "aplomb and dignity"[22] in the face of jokes, crude comments, and physical threats. Electrician and poet Susan Eisenberg was one of the pioneers. In a poem written ten years after she joined the union, she described the struggles to overcome the challenges she faced when she "walked into their party uninvited / wedging a welcome mat in the doorway." She finally left the trade without explaining her reasons to the surprised men she had worked with. They had come to accept her, but "after all those years / hurling back cannonballs / womanizing the barricades / firing only if she saw the whites of their eyes / it was the lonesomeness / of pioneering / that broke her resistance."[23]

Despite the resistance, unions were and are the most practical vehicle for women to enter the trades. A study based on 1989–91 apprenticeship data concluded that the share of women in all training programs was "very low," but the overwhelming majority of those few women who did achieve journey level status came out of union programs.[24] Since then, there has been a proliferation of union tradeswomen organizations and support groups for recruitment and retention. Some of the women entrants are military veterans, but almost all rise from low-waged service jobs. As a result of the substantial elevation of living standards, women tend to be among the most active and supportive of all union members. The number of women employed in the industry increased by 81.3% from 1985 to 2007 (prior to the Great Recession), reaching over one million total jobs, yet three-quarters of those were managerial, professional, or administrative.[25] Women's share of all blue-collar jobs in construction rose from 2.5% in 1999 to 3.4% in 2018, climbing at a faster pace than total employment but still extremely small.[26]

The rapid growth of the Latino workforce added another dimension to the issues of organizing, diversity, and inclusion. A willingness to welcome non-union workers now had to include addressing cultural and linguistic differences. The complex national politics of immigration and guest worker programs only reinforced the traditional orientation of maintaining barriers and opposing policies that might expand the ranks of workers in the industry. As immigrant workers continued to surface on jobsites in the last decades of the twentieth century, many union leaders and members initially reacted negatively, concerned that the new workforce was simply the latest ploy in the long campaign to undermine pay and safety standards. The fact that many of these workers were treated as independent contractors or paid in cash only added fuel to the fire, prompting calls for punitive deportation.

By and large, newly arrived Latino construction workers knew little about or mistrusted building trades unions, identifying them as part of a distant, alien, and hostile power structure. They turned to an alternate form of organization. A handful of worker centers were set up in the early 1990s and mushroomed to 137 by 2005. These centers are under-resourced service organizations that advocate for their members on both immigrant legal rights and worker rights. Unlike the hierarchical and formalistic building trades unions, workers centers are grassroots organizations with informal membership structures and improvisational cultures and strategies. They are typically funded by foundation grants, not members' dues.[27] In spite of (or perhaps because of) the structural differences, workers centers have demonstrated a capacity to operate effectively in a difficult environment.

The inevitable culture clashes occurred. Those locals that were prepared to recruit Latino workers frequently encountered hostility from the existing membership. In the summer of 2005, Las Vegas was in the midst of a boom and Hart Keeble, business manager of Ironworkers Local 416, was looking to fill 150 apprenticeship slots. Advertising in the mainstream press produced a handful of applicants, but the response soared when he contacted Spanish-language papers. The new recruits shifted the balance of his local from 80% native-born to one-half immigrant. The tensions between the two groups simmered and finally erupted when a brawl broke out at a union meeting.[28]

After the rocky beginnings, many unions now either accept or actively support workers centers in their communities, providing financial assistance, access to training, and political connections. Most existing union members are the children and grandchildren of immigrants. The new workforce is simply the latest wave of immigrants in construction. They are part of the workforce of the future, and servicing a shrinking pool of members can no longer suffice as a long-term strategy. Ken Rigmaiden, recently retired General President of the Painters Union, was the first African-American national leader of a building trades union. "We need to support our current members," Rigmaiden says, "but also support those workers who want to do the same work that we do—that means people of color and newly arrived workers to this country."[29]

Leveling top track of short wall.

9

Regulators and the Challenge of Enforcement

Payroll fraud has been recognized as both a cause and an effect of the decline of industry norms. Union leaders understood that their contracts' standards were threatened and that members were losing job opportunities to fraudulent contractors. Worker centers and immigrant advocacy groups lamented eroding pay, problematic safety conditions, and the exploitation of vulnerable workers. Other industry participants had a stake as well. Legitimate employers resented having to compete against firms that had gained an unfair competitive edge in an already highly competitive industry. Insurance companies noted the lost workers' compensation premiums. As the perspective on misclassification expanded to incorporate the gig economy, academics re-visited the public policy implications and resulting tax revenue losses when employers misclassified workers.

Unions sought solutions in local political arenas. In 1995, for example, the City Council of Cambridge, Massachusetts, passed a Responsible Employer Ordinance that further defined the word "responsible" in the phrase "low responsible bidder" that governed the awarding of contracts on publicly funded projects under the state's prevailing wage law. The ordinance spelled out a series of qualifying mandates for bidders, including a requirement to classify all workers on the project as employees rather than independent contractors. The intent of the law was to be proactive, that is, to prevent the award of a public project to an irresponsible contractor rather than relying on regulatory agencies to monitor violations once projects had been awarded. Dozens of communities around the country enacted similar legislation.

Union activists realized that an effective campaign to stop payroll fraud in construction required an analysis that the ramifications of the practice extended beyond its impact on union workers. Government policymakers considered the information provided by the various state studies on misclassification. Elected officials of both parties embraced the possibility of increasing revenues without raising taxes by escalating enforcement activity against illegitimate employers. It was difficult to make a political case justifying cheating. In Massachusetts, the administration of Republican Governor Mitt Romney had authorized the state Division of Unemployment Assistance to open its records to a Harvard research team. In 2004, following the release of the study, Romney signed the Massachusetts Misclassification Law, a bill passed by a Democratic legislature that clarified previously conflicting statutes and codified the ABC test to determine employment status.

Federal enforcement agencies had failed to staunch the growth of misclassification and shown only moderate interest in addressing the problem. The IRS presumably had the authority and the responsibility to regulate aggressively as a matter of tax enforcement, but Congress' decision to enact Section 530 had constituted a virtual blessing of the business model. The combination of the IRS safe harbor rule and the decline in funding for the U.S. DOL's Wage and Hour Division (WHD) had lowered expectations of forceful action from any agency in the federal government. Between 1978 and 2008, the number of WHD inspectors was reduced from 1,343 to 709. At the same time, the number of establishments covered by the federal Fair Labor Standards Act increased by 112%.[1]

The diminishing threat of adequate federal policing of workplaces encouraged labor standards violations. As funding for inspectors dwindled, many agencies responded by pulling remaining staff off the streets and into their offices. The relocation of personnel produced a cultural change that emphasized a more passive complaint-based model of enforcement. As a result, employers had fewer apprehensions about authorities routinely looking over their shoulders. Investigators focused on responding to calls about violations from individual workers in a seemingly random variety of workplaces. By 2004, complaints triggered 78% of all inspections undertaken by WHD.[2]

The energy for innovation in enforcement devolved to the state level, especially in blue states where workers' rights remained a somewhat higher priority. Massachusetts Governor Deval Patrick had donned a hard hat and work boots during his 2006 campaign and accompanied union organizers to several job sites where he talked openly to workers who were being paid in cash. As a result of his direct exposure, Patrick established the Task Force on the Underground Economy involving nine state agencies with overlapping jurisdictions to ensure that if one agency had a case involving payroll fraud, all agencies would take up the case under their statutory authority.[3]

New York had launched the first state-level task force in 2007 and other states soon followed. A 2020 National Employment Law Project (NELP) policy brief suggested that twenty-eight states have established either a formal or informal interagency task force.[4]

Prior to her 2021 appointment as U.S. Deputy Secretary of Labor, Julie Su had led California's wage administration programs, first as the Labor Commissioner of the California Division of Labor Standards Enforcement (DLSE) and then as the state's Labor Secretary. In those positions, she prioritized enforcing wage theft and misclassification violations. "We are on the side of employers who play by the rules," said Su, "we are on the side of employees whose rights have been violated."[5] She accepted the concept of "co-enforcement," an approach in which governmental agencies collaborate with outside organizations, such as worker centers and unions, to maximize the expertise and knowledge of both sets of partners. In an era of limited public investigatory resources, state Labor Departments increasingly rely on unions, workers centers, community organizations, and high-road employers as sources of information about the industries the agencies monitor.[6]

The District of Columbia, California, and New York paved the way in addressing the issue of joint employment. California's legislature passed AB 1701 in 2018, a bill that holds general contractors liable for their subcontractor's wage theft violations. Similarly, New York Senate Bill 2766-C went into effect in 2022, imposing stringent reporting requirements and making general contractors responsible for the correct payments to all workers on a project, including those employed by subcontractors.[7] These laws provide a tool to uncover the underlying decision-making dynamics on construction sites where individual workers may be uncertain about the identity of their employer. On May 29, 2019, the California DLSE issued citations totaling $597,933 to Universal Structural Building Corporation (USBC) and an additional $68,657 to J. H. McCormick, Inc., USBC's general contractor. The agency's press release noted that "up-the-chain general contractors are now responsible for wage theft committed by their subcontractors on all construction projects in the state."[8] Employer organizations have routinely attacked attempts to impose joint employer liability. The National Association of Home Builders (NAHB) website's brief on immigration policy illuminates the hypocritical stance of recognizing the reality of multi-tier subcontracting while refusing to be accountable for the consequences. The post insists that any reform ensures that employers should not be responsible for "the employees of their subcontractors."[9]

The concept of co-enforcement has been particularly effective with building trades unions that have developed the capacity to track employment patterns on job sites and identify instances of misclassification and payroll fraud. Since 2003, the national United Brotherhood of Carpenters has employed a full-time staffer dedicated exclusively to addressing the challenges of the underground economy from a legal and political perspective and has trained regional staff members to build cases with local authorities. Many unions have hired organizers with multiple language skills and assigned them to develop relationships with non-union trades workers and workers centers in order to act as their advocates with enforcement agencies in cases of wage theft. The joint efforts have produced dozens of successful civil and criminal actions across the country.[10]

Authority over wage enforcement at the state level has historically rested with labor departments. An exception is Massachusetts where that responsibility is part of the state attorney general's portfolio but in recent years, other offices of state attorneys general and local district attorneys have entered the fray, bringing charges involving crimes against workers. They have used the tools of the criminal justice system to prosecute cases of wage theft, misclassification, and payroll fraud. In some cases, dedicated units have been created, enabling lawyers to develop expertise in both labor and criminal law. Establishing a dedicated unit can institutionalize the work within an office, making it more likely that the mission will continue beyond the term of the particular attorney general or district attorney who initiated the activity. In just one example, the New York state attorney general obtained guilty pleas in 2018 to grand larceny and falsifying business records from three construction companies that had misclassified their workers as independent contractors to avoid paying overtime and unemployment insurance taxes.[11]

In 2014, David Weil was appointed head of WHD. Author of the seminal *The Fissured Workplace*, Weil suggested that the fissuring of employment had increased incentives for noncompliance, particularly at the bottom of several levels of subcontractors or among small franchisees where profit margins were thin and competition was fierce. This newly emerging workplace created greater complexity in defining who was ultimately responsible for compliance with the laws, given the multiple organizations with a hand in setting working conditions. Further, workers who may be most willing to take the initiative to contact agencies about potential problems do not necessarily operate in the industries with the highest incidence of violations. Conversely, workers who are less likely to voice complaints are often immigrants, less skilled, and less educated, and tend to be in workplaces with a higher degree of informal work arrangements.[12] During his relatively brief tenure, Weil steered the DOL away from a complaint-based model toward a strategic enforcement orientation that targeted industries where evidence showed workers were most likely to be mistakenly or deliberately cheated out of their wages with particular efforts to reach those sectors where workers were least likely to report such violations.

In 2015, WHD issued a far-reaching interpretative memorandum on misclassification that concluded, "Most workers are employees under the [Fair Labor Standards Act's] broad definitions"[13] (U.S. DOL 2015). The memorandum provided the intellectual and legal foundation for a heightened level of enforcement against employers who treated their workers as independent contractors in violation of the newly clarified DOL parameters. WHD entered into a series of memoranda of understanding on the issue of misclassification with multiple state agencies as well as the IRS and moved to ramp up enforcement programs. The resulting federal-state cooperation sparked hope for a reinvigorated era of labor standards protection. An Economic Policy Institute report, for example, claimed that $2 billion in stolen wages had been recovered for workers in 2015 and 2016 as a result of actions by the U.S. DOL, state Departments of Labor and attorney generals, and class action settlements.[14]

The brakes were applied when federal enforcement was severely curbed as part of President Trump's campaign to weaken or eliminate initiatives undertaken in nearly every arena of public policy during the Obama presidency. The federal government's stance on misclassification underwent a complete reversal. In 2017, Secretary of Labor Alexander Acosta withdrew the 2015 guidelines on independent contracting, removed the interpretative memorandum from the department's website, and curtailed federal investigations of cases involving misclassification.[15] The Trump administration proceeded to further loosen constraints on employers' ability to characterize their workers as independent contractors.

On April 16, 2019, the Trump-appointed general counsel of the National Labor Relations Board (NLRB) waded into the long-standing dispute over the correct classification for ride-sharing services by determining that Uber drivers were independent contractors rather than employees.[16] Two weeks later, in response to a request from a virtual marketplace company, the U.S. DOL issued an opinion letter on April 29 concluding that the workforce of a firm that operates in the "on-demand" or "sharing" economy should be considered independent contractors, not employees.[17] In August 2019, the NLRB held that misclassification of an employee does not constitute an unfair labor practice.[18] These directives generated by Trump labor officials widened a growing gulf between federal and state agencies tasked with similar missions. While the leadership at the U.S. DOL and the NLRB sought to minimize the importance of misclassification as an enforcement priority, many state labor standards agencies substantially increased their focus on the issue over the past decade.[19]

Ironically, in the same month that the Trump NLRB and DOL released their positions on the status of Uber and other on-demand workers, officials in several states announced plans to take an alternate path, ramping up efforts to combat misclassification. On April 15, 2019, Wisconsin Governor Tony Evers signed an executive order to form the Joint Enforcement Task Force on Employee Misclassification, and Montana Governor Steve Bullock issued an executive order to create the Task Force on Integrity in Wage Reporting and Employee Classification.[20] One week later, Michigan Attorney General Dana Nessel established the Payroll Fraud Enforcement Unit.[21] If the formation of these new bodies did not sufficiently indicate divergent paths, a statement by New Jersey Department of Labor Commissioner Rob Asaro-Angelo amplified the chasm between federal and state agency interpretations of their respective legal responsibilities when he said "[the DOL] opinion letter has zero effect on how the New Jersey Department of Labor enforces state laws."[22] Seven months later, the New Jersey Department of Labor demanded that Uber pay $649 million in unpaid unemployment taxes as a result of misclassification.[23]

Other state and even local regulatory bodies have expanded their efforts. In September 2019, Manhattan District Attorney Cyrus R. Vance Jr. announced the indictment of labor broker Salvador Almonte Jr. on multiple fraud charges stemming from a scheme that resulted in the underpayment of approximately $1 million of workers' compensation insurance premiums.[24] Vance's successor, District Attorney Alvin Bragg, issued an indictment against four construction companies, their owners, and a manager, for conspiracy to evade more than $1.7 million in workers' compensation insurance premiums over five years by creating a $20 million, off-the-books, cash payroll.[25] Minnesota's Hennepin County District Attorney adopted the legal theory of human trafficking to charge a contractor with the exploitation of immigrant construction workers, and the Louisiana Workforce Commission won a grand jury indictment of a drywall contractor for misclassification resulting in $794,000 in insurance fraud.[26] In July 2020, the Massachusetts Attorney General filed suit in Superior Court seeking a declaratory judgment that Uber and Lyft drivers are employees under the state's misclassification law.[27]

For many years, misclassification had occurred most frequently in the basic construction trades that had a tradition of piecework payments. Treating employees as independent contractors was less common within the mechanical trades as licensing requirements tended to promote conventional conditions of employment. But misclassification has come to permeate every corner of the industry. In January 2020, the attorney general of the District of Columbia reached a $2.75 million settlement with Power Design, Inc., a large national electrical contractor, for wage theft and misclassification. The lawsuit accused the Florida-based firm and two Maryland labor brokers of failing to "classify at least 535 electrical workers as employees in a scheme to cut costs and avoid legal responsibilities" on more than ten projects in the District. "If you cheat workers out of wages and benefits they've earned, or commit payroll fraud to gain an unlawful edge," said Attorney General Karl Racine, "you will be held accountable."[28]

In April 2022, Racine's office announced it had reached a settlement with drywall contractor Dynamic Contracting to pay $1,075,070 to resolve allegations that it avoided providing overtime pay and paid sick leave by misclassifying over 450 workers on construction projects throughout the District of Columbia. The settlement involved restitution to the workers, compensation to the District, and a set of policies and procedures to ensure future compliance.[29] Targets of the original lawsuit included four of Dynamic's labor subcontractors as well as two of Dynamic's general contractors—Gilbane Building Company and Consigli Construction Company. Interestingly, both Gilbane and Consigli work under collective bargaining agreements in stronger union geographical jurisdictions. Their use of Dynamic is one more indication of the segmentation of the industry. General contractors that work in multiple markets routinely put their fingers in the wind to determine what practices are acceptable and adjust their selection of subcontractors accordingly.

The emergence of the gig economy has altered the perception of independent contracting. Active regulatory agencies have come to consider misclassification in construction an illegal scheme, an obvious violation of employment laws. Those workers who are treated as independent contractors on large construction sites are clearly working under the direction and control of others. The barrier to eradication of the practice has been the political will and resources to enforce the laws, not a matter of legal interpretation. Gig employers, however, have promoted independent contracting as a desirable alternative to the dreary rat-race of employee wage slavery rather than a cost-saving and illegal method of employment that eliminated workers' rights. As the founder of Pasona, one of the world's largest temporary staffing agencies, said in 2007: "Be a regular worker—and be exploited for the rest of your life." As an alternative, he proposed the life of an independent contractor, which supposedly offered the allure of independence, individualism, flexibility, and entrepreneurialism. The ideological spin attempted to transform independent contracting from an obligation-evading scam into a transcendent model for twenty-first-century employment. The managing director of a nonprofit school charged with teaching low-income workers how to develop skills for the new sharing economy told the *San Francisco Chronicle* in 2017: "Everyone can be their own CEO."[30]

Given the perception of construction as an archaic industry, resistant to change and largely untouched by the wonders of technology, ridesharing and other forms of platform work have been promoted as harbingers of the future both in terms of algorithmic sophistication and the underlying organization of labor. In this view, independent contracting is a practice to be embraced, not eradicated. The pervasive influence of Silicon Valley's gig employers has muddied the waters of wage enforcement. Enforcement officials who had been comfortable going after construction violators in cases where the behavior was clearly unlawful have been skittish about taking on similar cases against the politically influential tech companies. Lobbyists for Uber, Lyft, and other ride share firms have successfully exempted their workforce from employment laws in a number of states through legislative action. In 2019, California passed AB 5, a bill that codified a judicial ruling setting the ABC test as the basis for determining who was an employee and who was an independent contractor. The ride share companies quickly mobilized, spending a record-breaking $200 million to pass Proposition 22, a 2020 ballot initiative that carved out their drivers from AB 5's jurisdiction.

The tech companies' use of independent contracting has put the issue of misclassification front and center in national policy debates. Misclassification has even emerged as an issue in the Covid era as management consultants advised clients to shift their employees to independent contractor status in order to avoid complying with vaccine mandates.[31] In his 2020 presidential campaign, Joe Biden condemned the various forms of payroll fraud and his platform promised "an aggressive, all-hands-on-deck enforcement effort that will dramatically reduce worker misclassification."[32] He announced his support for the PRO Act, the labor law reform proposal that would establish the ABC test as the law of the land under the National Labor Relations Act. While the PRO Act has languished in Congress, Secretary of Labor Marty Walsh announced the withdrawal of the Trump DOL's Independent Contractor rule in May of 2021 and two months later rescinded the Department's joint employer rule.[33] In addition, the National Labor Relations Board (NLRB) under Biden-appointee Jennifer Abruzzo as General Counsel, has inserted itself into the discussion. On March 17, 2022, one of the Board's Regional Directors issued a complaint charging several large transportation and logistics companies that operate out of the ports of Los Angeles and Long Beach with having informed "misclassified employee-drivers that they are independent contractors."[34] The practice of misclassification of truck drivers has been a crippling consequence of the deregulation of the trucking industry dating back to the Motor Carrier Act of 1980.

The road to enhanced enforcement, however, has been bumpy at the federal level. In March 2022, a Texas federal court ruled that the DOL's withdrawal of the independent contractor rule was unlawful, effectively leaving the Trump-era opinion intact. More significantly, the Biden administration's attempt to re-install David Weil as administrator of the Wage and Hour Division came to an unexpected halt on the floor of the Senate on March 30. The International Franchise Association led an intense business lobbying campaign, accusing Weil of being the "intellectual godfather" of joint employer rules holding parent corporations accountable for franchisees' labor practices. Democratic Senators Kyrsten Sinema, Joe Manchin, and Mark Kelly, who had been expected to support the nomination, instead voted with all fifty Republicans to torpedo Weil's candidacy. "I do not believe that the health and well-being of our small businesses and the employees who rely on their success would be his utmost priority," said Manchin in a statement following the vote.[35]

Enforcement in states with watchful agencies has served as a counterweight, limiting the expansion of payroll fraud. As in any other form of law enforcement, the protection of labor standards is a constant cat-and-mouse game between those who violate and those who administer the laws. From an enforcement perspective, the long-term goal is to deter rather than punish selective instances of illegal behavior, but chasing unlawful employers is usually a matter of playing catch up. From an employer perspective, the decision to misclassify workers in construction has always been a straightforward business matter—assessing the financial trade-off between the savings realized from labeling workers independent contractors versus suffering the potential penalties if caught. For many years, the answer was simple. The extension of payroll fraud into nearly every corner of the industry provided a competitive advantage to those who did not play by the rules.

Some contractors have modified their employment strategies by instituting a hybrid model consisting of a core of employees and a periphery of non-employees in order to deflect the spotlight of oversight. In areas with strong building trades unions and workers centers as well as sympathetic state administrations, companies that once classified all their workers as independent contractors now operate with a smaller group of employees and thereby nominally meet the legally required tax and insurance obligations. Once projects are in full swing and additional workers are needed, however, these contractors often turn to labor brokers who pay in cash. If questioned, the company of record can demonstrate compliance to authorities while the labor brokers are carried in the books as vendors or lower tier subcontractors with an invisible workforce. Solving this puzzle requires extensive investigatory legwork and forensic accounting to identify the misclassified workers—resources that even the most aggressive state agencies may be lacking.

For every contractor that chooses to "go straight," other non-union firms continue to play in the swamp of the underground economy, driven by the imperatives of success that depend on underbidding their competition through lower labor costs. Attorney Simon Leeming spent most of his early career helping construction employers that worked in Massachusetts to expand their use of independent contractors. He now points to union campaigns, the passage of the independent contractor bill in 2004, and a succession of pro-union state attorneys general as the reasons he has altered his legal advice. "The companies that I continued to represent," he claimed, "have their own employees predominantly." Yet Leeming acknowledged that "as the jobs change and as the labor needs change, they will go out and get work from labor [brokers]."[36]

Many employers that continue to play by the rules recognize the competitive challenge they face. In 2019, Matthew Townsend, president of the Signatory Wall and Ceiling Contractors Alliance, testified before a congressional committee: "In my industry, misclassification is not about making tough calls applying complicated laws to ambiguous facts. Rather, it is a choice simply to disregard wage and hour laws, workers' compensation laws, unemployment insurance regulations, and other basic responsibilities of being an employer. This is done for the purpose of gaining an advantage against law-abiding competitors, realizing tremendous profits, and avoiding the financial risks that honest entrepreneurs must accept. Business owners using the misclassification model do not bear the risks of unanticipated overtime, bad planning, or poor execution. Instead, this racket transfers these risks onto workers and taxpayers."[37]

Patricia Smith, a veteran of the misclassification wars, is the senior counselor to Secretary of Labor Marty Walsh. She has been the labor bureau chief of the New York State Attorney General's office, the New York State Commissioner of Labor, and the U.S. DOL's Solicitor. Testifying before a New Jersey task force, she recommended that state enforcement agencies adopt the tactics of interagency cooperation, both in terms of data sharing and coordinated enforcement actions. In addition, Smith urged the development of a comprehensive media outreach infrastructure to inform the public and to encourage employer deterrence.[38] As long as employers continue to violate employment laws in an effort to gain a cost advantage, a level playing field in a highly competitive industry will remain in jeopardy. If owners select contractors to build their projects based on price alone, even the most well-conceived union organizing campaigns will falter in the face of the sheer economics of bidding predicated on illegal and unethical employment arrangements. An effective regulatory logic of deterrence in construction has to incorporate a sophisticated understanding of financial incentives and disincentives. The future conditions of work in the industry hinge, to some degree, on the prevailing political winds and the resulting policy and enforcement choices of both federal and state agencies.

Hard hat with stickers.

10

Restoring a Pathway
to the Middle Class

Aggressive activity on the part of federal and state regulatory agencies is a precondition to the creation of a more level playing field, but the ultimate burden of representing workers and elevating standards rests squarely on the shoulders of the unions. The complacency that dominated most leaders' mindsets during the decades of union hegemony has not yet been completely replaced by a new paradigm in a more challenging environment. At the level of organizational structure, the decline in membership did force unions to streamline and reduce the number of struggling local unions. The Carpenters, for example, established regional councils in the 1990s as intermediate bodies to reflect changing dynamics in the industry, to mirror an increasingly regionalized group of employer counterparts, and to replace the chaos of decentralized and sometimes contradictory decision making by autonomous local unions with a more uniform set of policies and guidelines across multiple states. Other International unions have merged small locals into larger big city-based unions. The advantages are obvious. Mergers eliminate the duplication of legal, accounting, and other outside professional services and reduce the expense of the union's real estate footprint. The union's priorities can be consistently broadcast across a broader region and the larger local's resources can be applied to the weaker areas where the needs are greatest. Centralization can come at a cost, however. The presence of a union storefront in a medium-sized town served as a physical reminder to developers and politicians that a group of organized workers must be taken into account as part of the fabric of the community. Centralized power can and has been abused. Managing the tension between the efficiencies of a streamlined operation and the democratic nature of local grass roots activity is as much art as science.

The issues of union structure and decentralization are even more stark at the broad industry level. Unlike many other countries in the world with a singular construction workers union, there are fifteen free-standing building trades unions in the United States that have, at times, treated each other as competitors as well as allies. The t-shirts, hard hat stickers, and other paraphernalia of craft identification build a strong sense of loyalty to each individual union and, to a lesser degree, to the union sector of the industry as a whole. The extent of jurisdictional disputes is exaggerated by industry observers but as the technology and organization of work evolves, there are infrequent but recurring conflicts between unions whose members are already concerned about unstable work opportunities. While there is a national building trades organization as well as local and state councils, their roles are generally restricted to political action and negotiating large project agreements. They are umbrella organizations, limited in authority and ability to resolve internal differences and, more important, largely unable to execute multi-trade, industry-wide growth strategies. The resources rest with the individual international unions. The internal political challenge of herding cats frequently impedes the necessity to act in a coordinated and sustained manner.

The structure and function of union organizations matter in terms of growth and renewal. Unrepresented workers need to know that unions are well-run, effective operations worth joining for their ability to deliver both a higher standard of living and a welcoming internal environment. Member support for an organizing culture is key to the unions' future prospects. Just as COMET began a process of transformation, the need to continually reinforce updated variations on that message must be incorporated into the unions' internal education programs. Many apprenticeship programs include courses on financial literacy so new members can plan for the cyclical nature of the industry. Some also have classes on labor history, labor education, and industry analysis. If unions are to organize the unorganized, they must energize and inform the already organized.

The very concept of organizing in construction has taken multiple forms over time. During the era of union hegemony, union leaders sought to organize the work, not the workers. They supported proposed developments and tried to ensure that the membership remained sufficiently small to guarantee access to jobs. In the inimitable words of the brusque and direct George Meany: "We didn't want the people . . . we merely wanted the work. So far as the people who were on the work were concerned, for our part they could drop dead."[1] Limiting entrants to the unions became counterproductive once non-union workers outnumbered union members. Organizing the work was fruitless if the result was to advance the interests of workers on those very projects who did not hold union books. Initially many leaders reacted to the loss of density by internalizing the owners' critique that excessive compensation had made union contractors non-competitive. Some unions accepted wage cuts or freezes during the 1970s and 1980s in an attempt to reduce the delta between union and non-union labor costs, presumably restoring a competitive balance. After eighty years of steady growth, union construction wages turned down from 1972 to 1996, falling even faster than manufacturing wages despite that sector's far greater vulnerability to the usual suspects of outsourcing and globalization.[2] Recognizing the tactic, non-union contractors simply followed suit and decreased wages in order to maintain their bidding advantage. The concessionary strategy largely failed, resulting in lowered conditions for workers across the board.

An alternate and preferable approach is to reduce the delta by raising the floor, improving non-union conditions and, thereby, making labor costs more comparable. Given the widely varying conditions in the industry, the elevation of standards can take discrete forms for different groups of workers—negotiating a better contract for union members; bringing union conditions to a non-union contractor through an organizing campaign; or recouping back wages for exploited non-union workers through the actions of regulatory agencies. Each of these cases represents a repudiation of concessionary bargaining as a route to create a more competitive bidding environment. Each improvement is a rejection of the race to the bottom and, instead, an embrace of a strategy of elevating the floor, wherever that floor may be. The ultimate objective of organizing has to be to increase market share in order to improve standards across the entire industry. The mission today is to organize both the workers and the work.

The North America's Building Trades Unions (NABTU) published a *Campaign Guide*, a comprehensive training manual for union staff in the construction industry. The guide includes case studies of effective organizing efforts, chapters on the do's and don'ts of the arcane aspects of construction labor law, and a clear perspective that meaningful organizing strategies have to go beyond simply "selling" the benefits of union presence on a project by project basis. The authors list four necessary elements of a "4 X 4" organizing campaign—mobilized union members, unrepresented workers, targeted contractors, and secondary players that have the ability to alter the behavior of the primary contractor target. The guide suggests that successful organizing depends on "the right combination of tactics woven together by the right strategy so that these four critical elements are aligned in ways that magnify the power and impact of each one of them."[3]

While there are occasional conventional NLRB elections in construction, they remain few and far between. Organizing a non-union contractor's workforce begins with the problematic identification of the potential bargaining unit. Some may be employees, some independent contractors, some part of a lower tier labor broker's crew. Even in the case of a fully legally compliant employer, the employees have inevitable turnover and those that remain move from site to site. Organizing a union at a factory, retail store, warehouse, or other fixed location is difficult enough, but at least the bargaining unit members are in the same place and interact every day, laying the foundation for the fundamentals of a campaign. Construction workers tend to operate in smaller teams, encountering all their fellow employees only over time, if at all. Ruben Colon of the New York City District Council of Carpenters contends that if a company has fifty workers on a site, ten to fifteen may be among the core workforce, and the rest are often temporary "fly-by" workers. Still, Colon insists that "all good organizing campaigns start from the bottom-up. The workers must own the fight."[4]

Organizing for a contract cannot exist in a vacuum. With some exceptions, unions operate with an area master agreement to which signatory employers are bound. It is the industry's long-standing tradition of sectoral bargaining. Any newly organized company would be expected to accept those terms and conditions. A concessionary contract would provide a competitive advantage, upsetting the delicate balance of the level playing field that holds the union sector together. Some collective bargaining agreements even have most favored nation clauses that prohibit a union from granting any but the terms of the basic contract. The language protects long-time union employers from having to compete against newly organized firms with a sweetheart deal. Further, even a campaign that wins the support of a majority of the workers may not succeed because the employer would prefer to close the business or restructure the company rather than swim in unfamiliar waters. A targeted subcontractor might not have relationships with the union-oriented general contractor universe, and the estimators and project managers may have no experience operating within the framework of a union contract. Years of bidding against similar non-union firms is not necessarily adequate preparation for the union setting.

Successful bottom-up organizing requires a whole-market approach or, to be more precise, a whole-submarket approach. If workers unionize one company in one submarket and elevate wages, general contractors can ignore the now higher bids from that subcontractor and reward their long-standing non-union competitors whose labor cost structure remains unchanged. On the other hand, if most of the non-union plumbers who work on multiunit residential projects in a certain geographical area simultaneously organize their companies, they will have transformed the competitive environment and forced the general contractors in that market to recognize the newly elevated area standard. The challenges are considerable. Workers at a critical mass of similarly situated contractors would need to achieve union agreements in concert. Many of the subcontractors are likely to be small—possibly even family businesses—complicating the use of oppositional tactics common in a successful traditional election. Most employers in any industry believe that becoming a union shop will damage their business. In construction, even though the work product may be similar, that leap can be the biggest decision a non-union contractor will ever make. A union firm on an island in a non-union sea will have trouble surviving.

As a result, bottom up organizing in construction is more likely to be long-term relationship building rather than election campaigns. An increasing number of building trades unions have hired multilingual organizers who put on their hard hats and walk onto non-union job sites every day, seeking to build connections. The open gates of construction sites sometimes allow access and the opportunity for conversation until supervisors realize what is happening. The universe of contractors and workers in a particular market niche is sufficiently small that, within a year or two of daily job-site visits, effective organizers will encounter the same workers on multiple projects and hopefully create bonds of trust. These conversations bear fruit on multiple tracks. Organizers need to understand the business practice of each of the contractors in their market in terms of pay levels, employee vs. independent contractor status, reliance on labor brokers, and satisfaction of the workforce. A common method of enhanced information gathering is "salting," a practice in which union members are asked to work for a non-union contractor to gather information and build relationships. Since most regulatory agencies have limited resources to put inspectors in the field, the intelligence that salting can provide is often the initial basis of a targeted investigation. Agency staff rely on evidence and documentation—such as depositions, affidavits, photocopies of pay stubs—that unions can collect to demonstrate misclassification, failure to pay the prevailing wage on a publicly funded project, or wage theft on a private development.

The regular visits also offer organizers an opportunity to assess the skill level of individual trades workers. For an organizer who comes from the trades, watching someone wield their tools and talking to them about their work makes evaluations straightforward. Contractors succeed or fail on the talents and productivity of their workers. If, as the organizing slogan goes, the intent is to "turn 'em or burn 'em"—that is, sign a particular non-union contractor to an agreement or hurt its business aspirations, one of the most effective methods is to recruit the foremen or lead workers individually into the union world, particularly if there is little likelihood of a successful company-wide campaign. The practice of "stripping" has two mutually reinforcing attributes. It deprives the contractor of its most reliable producers of value, and it brings additional capacity into the union fold. In a best-case scenario, stripping can tip the decision-making scales for a non-union firm since signing an agreement can potentially result in the return of recently departed valuable members of its workforce. In one of the peculiar aspects of construction, stripping only works if one or several union contractors partner with the union to accomplish organizing goals. The cooperation of the union firm is key. When an organizer convinces a non-union worker to leave a secure, if unsatisfactory, situation for an unknown but more lucrative option, a union contractor must be prepared in advance to hire and place the worker immediately. Dangling the tantalizing promise of a better life without the ability to make it happen will only engender disappointment and bitterness against the union.

Top-down organizing is a more common approach and takes different forms dependent on the degree of union strength in an area. This method consists of convincing industry players to participate in the union market— either lobbying a private owner or public entity to build an upcoming project with union workers or encouraging the owners of non-union firms to sign a collective bargaining agreement. In an area with medium to high union market share, promoting the value of union construction to an owner can work. Particularly for institutional owners like universities and hospitals that build for the long run, the selling points are a skilled, productive, and available workforce, sophisticated contractors, strong safety protocols, and the unions' political support through the approval process. For developers who are fixated on the bottom line, the hostile presence of vocal union members at local permitting and zoning boards can delay and extend the timeline of a project and tip the scales of profitability. The organizers' information gathering activities come in handy in public meetings and private negotiations. Presenting credible documented instances of payroll fraud by unscrupulous contractors that are being considered for a project can serve as an effective shaming device against construction users whose concern about reputation may outweigh an obsessive desire to drive down labor costs. Alliances with community groups opposed to a particular project can serve as a powerful joint expression of resistance. In many ways, influencing the outcome of every upcoming project is a mini-organizing campaign unto itself. The key to success in top-down organizing is early intervention. Unions need a comprehensive system to track projects from their infancy that allows staff to open a dialogue with owners long before contractor selection occurs.

An owner's agreement to work collaboratively with the unions can take multiple forms. The simplest is a verbal pledge to assign a specific upcoming project to a union general contractor that uses union subcontractors. When the owner is a repeat user of construction services, the adoption of a generic policy for construction labor relations can include a commitment to the ongoing use of union contractors or an acceptance of minimal standards for contractor selection, such as the application of area prevailing wages or responsible contractor language. While the latter options do not guarantee the choice of a union firm, they eliminate the participation of irresponsible contractors and create a more level playing field for bidding.

One popular tactic is the Project Labor Agreement (PLA), a contract between an owner/agency and the unions, most commonly used on large-scale projects where unlimited access to labor and a need to avoid schedule disruptions are paramount. Public PLAs date back to the 1930s and the Depression-era Hoover and Grand Coulee Dams, at a time when construction union participation was largely unquestioned. As the non-union sector grew, opposition to PLAs became a regular feature of the ABC's publicity machine. When the Biden administration issued an executive order in February 2022 calling for PLAs on large scale federally funded projects, the ABC immediately attacked the Order's "flawed rationale" in ignoring "marketplace realities."[5] While there are distinctions between what is legally permissible on private versus public PLAs, both essentially establish union conditions on the designated project. In 1993, the U.S. Supreme Court affirmed the right of a governmental agency to enter into a PLA when it rejected an ABC sponsored challenge in the "Boston Harbor" case. Non-union contractors can participate in public PLA projects as long as their workforce is compensated in accordance with union agreements. However, non-union firms are generally reluctant to expose their workers to union standards on PLA jobs knowing the inevitable disappointment that will accompany the return to previous compensation patterns on their run-of-the-mill projects.

PLAs have become the contemporary version of organizing the work, rather than organizing the workers. Unions leaders can become excessively reliant on PLAs as an alternative to the more difficult work of expanding the membership and contractor base through organizing non-union firms and workers. PLAs create important and valuable opportunities for existing members but nonetheless reinforce the status quo. In some locations, PLAs have evolved into Community Benefits (or Workforce) Agreements, documents that incorporate minority and female hiring goals and community gains, along with a commitment to use union labor. These more progressive variants of PLAs have the virtue of engaging community organizations in partnerships to secure good jobs and boost the diversity of the union ranks.

Convincing an owner in an area with lesser union market share is more complicated. Even a sympathetic owner that is sufficiently concerned about reputational issues to avoid subsidizing contractors that play in the underground economy will ask union staffers the obvious question: Who can build my project given the limited penetration of union firms in my geographical market? Once again, this form of top-down project organizing requires the active participation of union employers. Contractors tend to be creatures of habit, bidding on similar types of projects in areas they know. Their comfort level on any given project rests on a knowledge of the workforce, previous relationships with owners, other contractors, and material suppliers, as well as a familiarity with the nature of the competition. When unions seek to extend their influence into new submarkets and new locations, signatory contractors have to become part of a collaborative effort, agreeing to chase those opportunities, willing to take the inevitable business risk, and jointly promoting the value of union construction to skeptical owners. A top-down union outreach becomes a hollow gesture without the active presence of an employer partner to perform the work.

In areas with virtually no union presence, worker advocates have used parallel concepts to improve conditions in the industry. The Texas-based Workers Defense Project operates in an almost completely non-union environment with high incidences of wage theft and virtually no state regulatory enforcement. They have instituted a version of responsible employer principles, seeking to encourage private owners and local City Councils to adopt the Better Builder Program, a package of standards that includes a commitment to a living wage, OSHA-10 safety trainings, workers' compensation coverage, hiring goals from the U. S. Department of Labor and local craft training programs, and independent third-party onsite monitoring to ensure the standards are being met. A far cry from a full-throated PLA, the Better Builder Program has managed to impact $2 billion worth of public and private construction by starting with the reality of current conditions and incrementally raising the floor.[6]

Attempts to persuade contractors to sign a contract face similar hurdles. In strong markets, a non-union contractor's opportunity for growth may be limited by its inability to bid in the union world. Ambitious young contractors may view the unions' training programs, supply of skilled labor, and access to larger projects as vehicles to boost revenues and enhance their business profile. Yet those same potentially persuasive arguments have little value in a mixed or predominantly non-union market. A non-union contractor may be dissatisfied with the quality and availability of its workforce, the constant petty conflicts with general contractors, and the stress of an unprofessional environment, but still remain convinced that signing a union agreement would be an immediate death sentence, placing the firm in a hopeless situation vis-à-vis its regular competitors who did not take a comparable step. Ironically, the very same union firms that may be willing to act as partners in extending markets frequently discourage organizers from bringing new companies into the fold. On the one hand, they appreciate the elimination of a business model that threatens their own; on the other, they do not welcome the added competition. It is not just union workers that have sought to keep a lid on the number of their colleagues in order to protect and augment their own work prospects.

Construction unions are generally politically effective. At the national level, the combination of their standing within the broader labor movement and a conservative tilt has sustained support through Democratic and Republican administrations. The continued presence of so-called "Davis-Bacon Republicans" in Congress has long been a bulwark against outright repeal of the federal prevailing wage law despite repeated efforts by the more openly ideologically anti-union elements of their party. At the local level, construction unions have always been active participants in promoting job-creating projects. Since development policies are at the heart of a community's political life—what will be built and who will build it—the trades have always cultivated relations with municipal and state decision-makers. Candidates may welcome union endorsements but the active involvement of engaged members at rallies, demonstrations, picket lines, volunteer charitable activities as well as regular attendance at local planning meetings has a more enduring impact. As the demographics of urban areas have shifted and demands for racial justice and environmental awareness have gained traction, a blanket pro-development stance can be out of step with prevailing political sentiment. Nonetheless, those unions that continue to be a voice for working class concerns in addition to supporting diversity and responsible development can play an outsized influential role.

The decline of market share and corresponding reduction in power at the local level has prompted unions to seek allies to amplify their political voice, in particular with the community-labor alliances that have sprung up in cities around the country. The Los Angeles Alliance for a New Economy (LAANE) was formed in the 1990s to offer a medley of organizing initiatives, research, political action, and policy development. In 1998, the building trades cooperated with LAANE to negotiate a Community Benefits Agreement—a PLA with hiring and other community goals—on a Hollywood hotel, retail and theater project. Three years later, after a developer reneged on commitments to area building trades unions, joint labor and community pressure produced a CBA for the new Staples Center with union conditions, "first source" hiring for those displaced by the development, public park improvements and a commitment to affordable housing.[7] A subsequent campaign won a PLA/CBA on the city's transit jobs to secure union jobs and create a pathway for community residents to enter apprenticeship programs. Since then, the Los Angeles Building Trades and LAANE have fought together for affordable housing and green jobs. "We try to leverage the power that comes from community-labor alliances to win socially valuable projects with good union jobs," says Roxana Tynan, LAANE's Executive Director.[8]

Building trades union programs in the United States and Canada invest $1.5 billion to train half a million workers every year.[9] The content can range from brief OSHA safety courses to journey worker skill upgrade classes to full-fledged four-year registered apprenticeship programs. The quality and depth of the individual programs may vary, but the common thread is the recognition that enhanced skill and productivity is the ultimate justification for higher levels of compensation. While technology, prefabrication, and specialization may have reduced the need for highly skilled generalists, today's construction employers still depend heavily on the craft knowledge and technical abilities of their workforce. The most sophisticated programs train not only for all the traditional skills but anticipate the industry's future needs by incorporating courses on BIM, CAD, CNC, and green construction techniques in their curricula as well as scheduling product-specific sessions for contractors experimenting with new materials and methods.

Private sector construction apprenticeship training is one of the more enduring and effective models of introducing new entrants to the workplace. Overseen since 1937 by the federal National Apprenticeship Act, the programs are funded by a relatively small hourly contribution in collective bargaining agreements and designed to overcome a single employer's reluctance to spend aggressively on training, knowing that the prospective trainee might ultimately work for a competitor. By spreading the costs across a multi-employer universe, individual contractors know that they will eventually benefit from access to a pool of apprentices at a minimal cost. There is no similar national model in the non-union world of single atomized firms, a reality that has proven to be an Achilles' heel in developing a skilled workforce. There is relatively little published data on non-union training programs, making comparisons difficult. One study reviewed 2014 IRS 990 forms for small tax exempt non-profit organizations and found that non-signatory organizations involved in construction training had $242 million in assets contrasted to $2.7 billion in assets for non-profits associated with signatory organizations.[10]

From the apprentices' perspective, the "earn while you learn" model is far more appealing than the alternative of racking up student loan debt for an uncertain post-college future. Though not all union members start their careers as apprentices, the best barometer of the orientation of tomorrow's workforce is the composition of today's training programs. According to the NABTU Research Department, over three-quarters of the 3,500 graduates in the two hundred pre-apprenticeship programs around the country came from communities of color while the percentage of women averaged just under 25% from 2017–2022.[11] "We aggressively recruit non-traditional workers outside the conventional direct entry process by partnering with community organizations, pre-apprenticeship programs, and high schools," says Leah Rambo, director of the New York City Sheet Metal apprentice program. "Recruiting and maintaining a diverse workforce also involves training current members about appropriate behavior on the job, directly addressing the issue of racial and/or sexual harassment with zero tolerance policies."[12]

There are over a thousand multiemployer collectively bargained pension and annuity plans in construction with over $300 billion in assets.[13] These plans are also funded by hourly contributions negotiated in local collective bargaining agreements and then managed by an equal number of labor and management trustees. As with all pension plans, there are only a few levers to impact the financial well-being of the fund—the amount of the hourly contribution, the aggregate number of hours worked in a fiscal year, and the investment return. Federal oversight guidelines direct trustees to maximize risk-adjusted investment returns for the plans' participants as their overriding fiduciary duty. Within those boundaries, however, most construction funds have sought vehicles to combine good returns with job creation. Real estate investments usually constitute less than two percent of a typical portfolio across all multiemployer collectively bargaining plans but, in the construction realm, union plans often invest between ten and fifteen percent of the total funds in the real estate asset class with provisos that the money be used for union-built projects. A study done for the National Electrical Benefit Fund showed that by investing $6.25 billion in real estate between 2012 and 2020, the fund generated 34,528 construction jobs.[14] Given that the contributions are the members' deferred income, it is understandable that the concept of capital strategies, i.e., the targeted use of pension assets to support workers' rights and workers' opportunities while achieving appropriate returns, should advance their interests.

All of the building trades unions' benefit funds—apprenticeship, pension and annuity, and health—are administered jointly by labor and management trustees. While there are the standard face-offs during contract negotiations, the joint boards tend to be harmonious. In general, the notion of labor-management cooperation is more than just rhetoric in the construction industry. Management personnel among general contractors and construction managers are often college educated with degrees in civil engineering but subcontractors and their office staff frequently worked in the field earlier in their careers and maintain stronger cultural and social ties along with a respect for the trade skills. Pension and health trustees seek the best value for the dollars contributed to their funds, and apprenticeship trustees from both sides aim to provide the most comprehensive training programs they can afford. Open minded contractors at all levels recognize that the welfare of their business is connected to the effectiveness of the unions. Beyond their roles as management trustees, some employers understand and support the unions' organizing programs. If the union is able to extend its reach and increase market share, that creates more opportunities for individual employers. The combination of cultural and strategic commonalities can create the kind of respectful relations that result in effective joint efforts.

Off-shore wind farm turbines: clean energy jobs.

Carrying materials on the job.

11

Building a High Road Future

For the first three-quarters of the twentieth century—particularly in the three decades after World War II—U.S. construction workers were among the best paid blue-collar workers in the world. A career in construction was a pathway to the middle class for those "labor aristocrats." During the last fifty years, that era has been replaced by a segmented new equilibrium. Aggregate real wages for all workers have declined, but not evenly across the board. Union trades workers make up a smaller percentage of the total construction workforce, but they continue to earn above average wages and benefits. Some non-union contractors that operate in unionized markets or that need specialized skills pay less but remain within shouting distance of the union scale. The conditions on the vast majority of non-union projects, however, are a pale reflection of a once proud industry. Wages are low, benefits are non-existent, wage theft is not uncommon, the underground economy is a looming presence, and safety is frequently compromised. OSHA conducted eleven investigations into construction-related fatalities in New York City in 2020. All were at nonunion sites.[1]

Since construction is such a highly competitive, decentralized industry and contractors function with a short-term business horizon, a herd mentality rules the landscape. If one firm adopts new technology or introduces more efficient techniques into its business model, their peers are sure to follow for fear of losing out on upcoming bids. The same is true of labor practices. In the distant past when unions reigned supreme, a new employer entrant would automatically sign a collective bargaining agreement because that was the prevailing industry environment. Once cracks appeared in the union hegemonic system, however, when some portion of the contractors' universe in a particular submarket in a geographical area shifted their employees to independent contractor status or moved to pay in cash, others faced the unenviable choice of following their lead by descending on a downward compensation spiral or going out of business.

Returning to a uniformly higher standard is constrained by the very competitive dynamics that drove conditions down. No single contractor has a sufficiently sizable guaranteed backlog of work that would allow a unilateral decision to elevate standards as long as competitors refused to desert their problematic practices. Winning comprehensive improvements requires a whole-market approach using the full toolbox of methods. Regulatory agencies have to enforce employment laws and worker advocacy groups—whether they be unions or worker centers—must organize to move overall conditions up the ladder. Strategic top-down and bottom-up organizing can maintain and extend market share. An active and engaged membership can inject energy into political and policy discussions. Community Benefit Agreements and community-labor alliances help secure union jobs while adding diversity to the union ranks. Anticipating and preparing for future industry developments, such as increased off-site prefabrication and modularization, green construction, and specialization, can guide training programs' curricula to maintain a productivity edge. Leveraging pension assets with a capital strategies approach is not a silver bullet but can be a supplemental job-creating tool.

The notion of responsible employer principles can be used in every area, regardless of the presence or absence of unions. Solid collective bargaining agreements, responsible employer ordinances and PLAs in strong union markets, and the Better Builder Program in non-union Texas may seem entirely separate methods in specific terms and conditions. Yet all of them attempt to establish a floor for permissible employer practices and ban the unscrupulous contractor model that has so severely damaged the industry. The concepts are similar, i.e., to establish the parameters of acceptable contractor behavior that will, step-by-step, either sustain or return dignity and respect to the workforce. Construction workers should be rewarded fairly for their willingness to perform dangerous tasks, and the universal pathway to the middle class should be reinvigorated. Construction workers build the physical fabric of our society and deserve recognition for their contribution. As Emily Timm of the Workers Defense Project suggests, "It's pretty basic. Workers should be safe on the job, be paid a dignified wage and benefits, have the ability to set standards, and have a voice."[2]

Despite the challenges of off-site production, specialization, deskilling, and technological advances, there will continue to be a need for skilled construction workers on job sites. Perhaps the levels of individual autonomy and problem-solving talents will be less than a century ago, but the basic mastery of crafts will continue to be important, necessary, and satisfying. The demand for residential and non-residential products is unceasing and new types of construction will likely emerge. As clean energy projects create job opportunities, groups like the labor-led Climate Jobs National Resource Center can help overcome the sometimes contentious relationship that existed between building trades unions and environmental groups. The CJNRC's mission is to educate workers about and advocate for climate policies that will build a clean energy economy, create good union careers, and impact racial and economic inequality, one more expression of the kind of community labor partnerships that have appeared in the last twenty years.

Like many others, my union contains the word Brotherhood in its full name. Apart from the obvious gender bias, there is significance and a rich history in the use of that word. Building trades unions have been and still are more than just the equivalent of worker insurance companies that negotiate and administer wage and benefit programs and refer workers to jobs. They do function as collective bargaining and member servicing instruments, but they are also social organizations that create a bond of identification based on trade. Craft pride is not simply a matter of an individual's grasp of a set of skills but includes, in addition, a sense of belonging to a team of men and women with comparable levels of competence. On the one hand, there is a competitive dynamic between individual workers seeking a finite number of jobs in a given area. On the other, there is the collegial connection of a shared employment experience and the possibility of working alongside most other members at some point during an extended career. Many members simply go to work, go home, and live their private lives, but a significant number identify more strongly with their craft and their union. They attend union meetings and annual holiday parties for the social connection as much as for the information presented from the podium.

Concern over competition for jobs fluctuates with the industry's business cycles. During a downturn, every opportunity is precious and the end of a job triggers apprehension about future paychecks. During a boom, workers can be more cavalier, knowing there is probably another prospect around the corner. The overriding connecting link during good and bad times is the remarkable reality that every union journey worker of a given trade on any particular job is entitled to the exact same hourly pay and benefits under the collective bargaining agreement. Unlike most other occupations, union trades workers walk into a new job knowing in advance that their wages have been established and knowing that figure will be the same as their co-workers. The stress of individual salary negotiations with an employer and the potential resentment of others doing similar tasks with disparate pay levels are absent. That transparency and collectively bargained equality is the foundation of the brotherhood/sisterhood of union members.

These social bonds have frayed along with the decline in union density over the last fifty years. There is little to be gained by a return to the traditions of the past with all of the limitations and exclusionary practices of country club unionism. Construction work remains one of the few remaining blue-collar occupations that can be both psychologically fulfilling and financially rewarding when workers are treated with the dignity and respect they deserve. Trades workers literally build our communities, yet only those fortunate enough to be union members can hope for the comforts of a secure livelihood. Peter McGuire founded the Carpenters Union in 1881. His enduring motto was "Organize, Agitate, Educate." There is no reason why a high-road model of building trades unionism cannot evolve from the best practices of the past—the sense of craft pride, the commitment to training, and the effectiveness of sectoral multiemployer bargaining—with a renewed commitment to organizing, diversity, and an activist membership.

Attaching spreaders to the hook of a crane.

Notes

Chapter 1. A Tale of Two Cities

1. Mark Turpin, *Hammer: Poems* (Louisville, KY: Sarabande Books, 2003), 33.

2. Bureau of Labor Statistics Current Employment Statistics (www.bls.gov/ces).

3. Eugene Friedmann and Robert Havighurst, *The Meaning of Work and Retirement* (University of Chicago Press, 1954), 172.

4. Herbert Applebaum, *Royal Blue: The Culture of Construction Workers* (New York: Holt, Rinehart, and Winston, 1981), 22, 11.

5. Mary Bedell, Employment and Income of Negro Workers—1940–52, *Monthly Labor Review*, June 1953: 598–99.

6. Joel Seidman, Jack London, Bernard Karsh, and Daisy Tagliacozzo, *The Worker Views His Union* (University of Chicago, 1958), 50.

7. Studs Terkel, *Working* (The New Press, 1972), 27.

8. Mark Erlich, *With Our Hands: The Story of Carpenters in Massachusetts* (Philadelphia: Temple University Press), 1.

9. Erin Johansson and Benjamin Woods, "*Building Career Opportunities for Women and People of Color: Breakthroughs in Construction*," JwJ Education Fund and NABTU Tradeswomen Committee, November 2016, 23.

10. Gabriel Pleites and Peter Philips, "And All the Plenty Shall Be Forgotten: 80 Fat and 50 Lean Years of Construction Union Wages," [unpublished paper] 2022.

11. US Bureau of Labor Statistics, Employment, Hours, and Earnings from the Current Employment Statistics survey (National).

12. William Haber and Harold Levinson, *Labor Relations and Productivity in the Building Trades* (Bureau of Industrial Relations, University of Michigan, 1956), 35.

13. unionstats.com.

14. Leo Troy, *U.S. Union Source Book: Membership, Finances, Structure, Directory* (IRDIS, 1985), 3–15.

15. http://www.unionstats.com.

16. Frank Manzo and Erik Thorson, *Union Apprenticeships: The Bachelor's Degrees of the Construction Industry*, Illinois Economic Policy Institute, September 7, 2021, 6.

17. Ken Jacobs, Kuochih Huang, Jenifer MacGillvary, and Enrique Lopezlira, "The Public Cost of Low-Wage Jobs in the US Construction Industry," UC Berkeley Center for Labor Research and Education, January 2022.

18. Gomez, interview, September 2020.

19. Beldi, interview, https://www.youtube.com/watch?v=n-Nb88S1WDg, 2014.

20. Minyvonne Burke, "Final remains recovered from Hard Rock Hotel site collapse in New Orleans," NBC News, August 18, 2020.

21. Jeffrey Passell and D'Vera Cohn, *Occupations of Unauthorized Immigrant Workforce*, Pew Research Center, November 3, 2016.

22. https://www.youtube.com/watch?v=otMpiOhVmxg.

23. Eli Rosenberg, "How a worker who survived a catastrophic building collapse ended up in ICE detention," *Washington Post*, November 25, 2019.

24. Number and rate of fatal work injuries, by industry sector (bls.gov).

25. New York Committee for Occupational Safety and Health, "Deadly Skyline: An Annual Report on Construction Fatalities In New York State," February 2022, 2.

Chapter 2. Snapshot of an Industry

1. William Haycraft, "History of Construction Equipment," *Journal of Construction Engineering and Management,* October 2011, 722.

2. https://www.bea.gov/sites/default/files/2022-03/gdp4q21_3rd.pdf.

3. https://data.census.gov/cedsci/table?q=workers%20by%20industry&t=Industry &tid=ACSDT1Y2019.B24070&vintage=2018. The use of the number 11 million is based on an estimate of *all* workers in the industry, i.e., employees, legitimate independent contractors, misclassified independent contractors, and those who are paid off-the-books.

4. Haber and Levinson, *Labor Relations and Productivity in the Building Trades*, 3.

5. U.S. Bureau of Labor Statistics www.bls.gov.

6. BEA Value added by Industry: http://apps.bea.gov/iTable/iTableHtml.cfm?req id=150&step=3&isuri=1&Table_List=1&SERIES=A&FIRST_YEAR=1997&Columns =II&SCALE=-9&LAST_YEAR=2021&categories=gdpxind&TheTable=&ROWS= 22R#.YmB81QIb6hQ

7. https://www.census.gov/construction/c30/historical_data.html.

8. https://www.statista.com/statistics/234153/the-largest-us-construction -contractors-based-on-contracting-revenue/.

9. U.S. & states, 60 digit NAICS excel, https://www.census.gov/data/tables/2019/ econ/susb/2019-susb-annual.html.

10. Haber and Levinson, *Labor Relations and Productivity in the Building Trades*, 24.

11. U.S. Census Bureau, 2012 Economic Census, Survey of Business Owners.

12. William A. Starrett, *Skyscrapers and the Men Who Build Them* (New York: Scribner's, 1928), 288.

13. See David Weil, "The Contemporary Industrial Relations System in Construction: Analysis, Observations and Speculations," *Labor History* 46, no. 4 (November 2005).

Chapter 3. The Heavy Hand of the Business Roundtable

1. Thomas O'Hanlon, "Unchecked Power of the Building Trades," *Fortune* 78, no. 7 (December 1, 1968): 102.

2. U.S. Bureau of Labor Statistics, 1975, "Work stoppages in contract construction, 1962–73," Bulletin 1847, Washington, DC: U.S. Department of Labor.

3. "BNA Construction Labor Report," Bureau of National Affairs newsletter, 1970.

4. Marc Linder, *Wars of Attrition: Vietnam, the Business Roundtable, and the Decline of Construction Unions* (Iowa City, IA: Fanpihua Press, 2000).

5. Business Roundtable, "More Construction for the Money: Summary Report of the Construction Industry Cost Effectiveness Project." January 1983, 12, 29.

6. "BNA Construction Labor Report," Bureau of National Affairs newsletter, November 20, 1968.

7. Stanley Goldhaber, Chandra K. Jha, and Manuel C. Macedo, Jr., *Construction Management: Principles and Practices* (New York: John Wiley & Sons, 1977), ix.

8. Gerhard Bosch and Peter Philips, eds., *Building Chaos: An International Comparison of Deregulation in the Construction Industry* (New York: Routledge/Taylor & Francis, 2003).

9. Sidney Levy, *Project Management in Construction* (New York: McGraw-Hill, 2000), 6.

10. See David Weil, *The Fissured Workplace: Why Work Became So Bad for So Many and What Can Be Done to Improve It* (Cambridge, MA: Harvard University Press, 2014).

11. US Department of Labor, Wage and Hour Division, "Dollar threshold amount for contract coverage," January 1, 2022.

12. Mark Erlich, *Labor at the Ballot Box: The Massachusetts Prevailing Wage Campaign of 1988* (Philadelphia: Temple University Press, 1990).

13. Andrew Kessler, "Independent Contractor Safe-Harbor Rules Await Congressional Amendment," *Tax Lawyer* 47, no. 4 (1994): 1077–88.

14. Franco Ordonez and Mandy Locke, "IRS 'safe harbor' loophole frustrates those fighting labor tax cheats," McClatchy Washington Bureau, December 14, 2014. Accessed at https://www.mcclatchydc.com/news/nation-world/national/economy/article24777397.html.

15. U.S. Government Accountability Office, "Employee misclassification: Improved coordination, outreach, and targeting could better ensure detection and prevention," GAO-09-717, August 10, 2009. Accessed at https://www.gao.gov/products/GAO-09-717.

16. Ordonez and Locke, "IRS' 'safe harbor' loophole frustrates those fighting labor tax cheats."

Chapter 4. Misclassification as a Business Model

1. Audrey Freedman, "How the 1980s Have Changed Industrial Relations," *Monthly Labor Review* 111, no. 5 (1988): 35.

2. Loren Steffy and Stan Marek, *Deconstructed: An Insider's View of Illegal Immigration and the Building Trades* (College Station: Texas A&M Press/Stoney Creek Publishing Group, 2020).

3. Steffy and Marek, *Deconstructed*.

4. "BNA Construction Labor Report," Bureau of National Affairs newsletter, April 28, 1999.

5. *Engineering News-Record*, June 3, 2013, 10.

6. Peciaro, interview, March 2020.

7. U.S. Bureau of the Census, 1985, "1982 Census of Construction Industries: U.S. Summary: Establishments With and Without Payroll," Washington, DC: U.S. Department of Commerce.

8. "Investigation in Utah and Arizona Secures Wages and Benefits for More Than 1,000 Construction Workers Who Were Wrongly Classified," US Department of Labor, April 23, 2015; "Paul Johnson Drywall Inc. Agrees to Pay $600,000 in Back Wages, Damages and Penalties Following US Labor Department Investigation," US Department of Labor, May 19, 2014.

9. Simon Leeming, attorney at Preti Flaherty, Boston, in an interview by the author, July 27, 2018.

10. Charles Seeman, Edward Hennessey, and Richard Cooper (eds.), *The Construction Lawyer's Guide to Labor and Employment Law* (Chicago: American Bar Association, 2001).

11. "BNA Construction Labor Report," Bureau of National Affairs newsletter, Jan. 2, 2002.

Chapter 5. Immigration, Payroll Fraud, and the Underground Economy

1. Louis Hyman, *Temp: How American Work, American Business, and the American Dream Became Temporary* (New York: Viking, 2018), 252.

2. *U.S. News & World Report*, "Crackdown on illegal aliens—the impact," July 2, 1984.

3. Rakesh Kochhar, "The Occupational Status and Mobility of Hispanics," Pew Research Center, December 15, 2005.

4. "Construction Jobs Expand for Latinos Despite Slump in Housing Market," Pew Research Center, March 7, 2007.

5. Natalie Kitroeff, "Immigrants Flooded California Construction. Worker Pay Sank. Here's Why." *Los Angeles Times,* April 22, 2017.

6. Robert Warren, "US undocumented population drops below 11 million in 2014, with continued declines in the Mexican undocumented population," *Journal on Migration and Human Security* 4, no. 1 (2016): 1–15; Migration Policy Institute, n.d., "Profile of the Unauthorized Population: Texas," in Jeffrey Passell and D'Vera Cohn, "Occupations of Unauthorized Immigrant Workforce," Pew Research Center, November 3, 2016. https://www.migrationpolicy.org/data/unauthorized-immigrant -population/state/TX.

7. Jeffrey Passell and D'Vera Cohn, "Occupations of Unauthorized Immigrant Workforce," Pew Research Center, November 3, 2016.

8. Workers Defense Project, 2013, "Build a Better Texas: Construction Working Conditions in the Lone Star State," Workers Defense Project in collaboration with the Division of Diversity and Community Engagement at the University of Texas at Austin; Workers Defense Project, 2017, "Build a Better South: Construction Working Conditions in the Southern U.S.," Workers Defense Project and the Partnership for Working Families.

9. Gomez, interview, September 2020.

10. Florida Division of Insurance Fraud, Case No. 11-460, *Probable Cause Affidavit, Request for Arrest Warrant,* Defendants Hugo Otoniel Rodriguez, et. al., July 23, 2012, 12.

11. Demetria Kalodimos, "Is Music City Center Construction Funding 'Underground Economy?'" WSMTV Nashville, July 18, 2011, https://www.wsmv.com/ news/is-music-city-center-construction-funding-underground-economy/article _ea86e0f8-1d26-5b14-86e2-c4d82eee48b0.html.

12. Mike Reicher, "Special Report: Amid Nashville's Housing Boom, Safety Rules are Ignored and More Workers Die," *The Tennessean,* May 18, 2018.

13. Alejandro Ramirez, "Safety, Compensation and Accountability at Nashville Construction Sites," *Nashville Scene,* November 12, 2020.

14. Alejandro Ramirez, "New Bill Could Raise Standards for Awarding Construction Contracts, *Nashville Scene,* March 2, 2021; Stephen Elliot, "Nashville Worker-Safety Push 'Gutted' by New State Law," *Nashville Scene,* April 1, 2021.

15. "BNA Construction Labor Report," Bureau of National Affairs newsletter, March 26, 2003.

16. Oliver Cooke, Deborah Figart, and John Froonjian, "The Underground Construction Economy in New Jersey," Hughes Center for Public Policy, June 2016, 3; Yvonne Yen Liu, Daniel Flaming, and Patrick Burns, "Sinking Underground: The Growing Informal Economy in California Construction," Economic Roundtable, 2014, 2.

17. Steffy and Marek, *Deconstructed.*

18. "Non-U.S. Citizens Make Up 39% of NYC's Construction Workforce," *The Real Deal,* December 21, 2011; "The Underground Economy in the New York City

Affordable Housing Industry," Fiscal Policy Institute, April 17, 2007, http://fiscalpolicy.org/the-underground-economy-innew-york-citys-affordable-housing-construction-industry.

19. Leeming, interview, 2018.

20. National Carpentry Contractors, 1-RC-22133, decision and order of regional director, January 11, 2008.

21. *State of Minnesota v. Ricardo Ernesto Batres*, Court File No. 27-CR-18-24013, September 25, 2018, 3.

22. "Two Men Plead Guilty to Fraudulent Scheme to Evade Payroll Taxes and Workers' Compensation Requirements in Construction Industry," U.S. Attorney's Office, Middle District of Florida, March 30, 2021.

23. "Couple Pleads Guilty to Conspiracy to Commit Wire Fraud and Conspiracy to Impede and Defraud the IRS," U.S. Attorney's Office, Middle District of Florida, March 10, 2022.

24. "Through Layers of Subcontractors, An Inside Look at Greed and Exploitation," StopTaxFraud.net, 2022, https://stoptaxfraud.net/through-layers-of-subcontractors-an-inside-look-at-greed-and-exploitation.

25. Capece, interview, March 2022.

26. Lynn Bonner, "Construction Sites are 'High-Risk' Settings for Coronavirus Infection, NC Official Says," *Raleigh News & Observer*, June 15, 2020, https://www.newsobserver.com/news/local/article243550137.html.

27. David Weil and Amanda Pyles, "Why Complain? Complaints, Compliance, and the Problem of Enforcement in the U.S. Workplace," *Comparative Labor Law & Policy Journal* 27, no. 1 (2005): 59–92.

28. Francoise Carre and Randall Wilson, "The Social and Economic Costs of Employee Misclassification in Construction," Harvard Labor and Worklife Program report, 2004.

29. Tennessee Bureau of Workers' Compensation, *Annual Report on Employer Coverage Compliance* 6 (February 1, 2019), https://www.tn.gov/content/dam/tn/workforce/documents/injuries/2019ComplianceAnnualReport.pdf.

30. Russell Ormiston, Dale Belman, and Mark Erlich, "An Empirical Methodology to Estimate the Incidence and Costs of Payroll Fraud in the Construction Industry," 2020 report, http://stoptaxfraud.net/wp-content/uploads/2020/03/National-Carpenters-Study-Methodology-for-Wage-and-Tax-Fraud-Report-FINAL.pdf.

31. Gilbert Burck, "A Time of Reckoning for the Building Unions," *Fortune* 99 (June 4, 1979): 82–85.

32. *Engineering News-Record*, December 15, 1982, 132.

33. Haber and Levinson, *Labor Relations and Productivity in the Building Trades*, 35.

34. Steven Allen, "Developments in collective bargaining in construction in the 1980s and 1990s," NBER Working Paper No. 4674, National Bureau of Economic Research, 1994.

35. Mark Erlich and Jeff Grabelsky, "Standing at a Crossroads: The Building Trades in the Twenty-First Century," *Labor History* 46, no. 4 (2005): 421–45.

36. "BNA Construction Labor Report," Bureau of National Affairs newsletter, August 15, 2001.

37. U.S. Chamber of Commerce, Commercial Construction Index, Q3 2021, 5.

38. Becky Schultz, "Lack of Skilled Construction Labor is a Real Threat to Housing Supply and Affordability," ForConstructionPros.com, November 15, 2021.

39. Zachary Phillips, "Construction's Career Crisis: How Did We Get Here?" *Construction Dive*, October 20, 2021.

40. Zachary Phillips, "High Pay Attracts Workers, but Construction's Employment Gap Widens," *Construction Dive*, June 9, 2022.

Chapter 6. Technology and the Future of Construction Work

1. Adam Smith, *Wealth of Nations* (Freebook Publisher, 2000), 5; John Maynard Keynes, "Economic Possibilities for Our Grandchildren," *The Nation & Athenaeum*, October 18, 1930.

2. Richard M. Cyert and David C. Mowery, eds., *Innovation and Growth in the U.S. Economy* (Washington, DC: National Academy Press, 1987), 4; MIT Work of the Future Task Force, *The Work of the Future: Building Better Jobs in an Age of Intelligent Machines* (MIT Press, 2020), 4.

3. Carl Benedikt Frey and Michael A.Osborne, "The Future of Employment: How Susceptible are Jobs to Computerisation?" Oxford University Press, 2013; https://www.oecd.org/future-of-work/Future-of-work-infographic-web-full-size.pdf; McKinsey Global Institute, "A Future That Works: Automation, Employment, and Productivity," January 2017, 8; World Economic Forum, "The Future of Jobs Report 2020," October 2020, 5; Erin Winnick, "Every Study We Could Find on What Automation Will Do to Jobs, in One Chart," *MIT Technology Review*, January 25, 2018.

4. Karen Harris, Austin Kimson, and Andrew Schwedel, "Labor 2030: The Collision of Demographics, Automation and Inequality," Bain & Company, February 7, 2018, 21, 26.

5. Jill Manzo, Frank Manzo, and Robert Bruno, "The Potential Economic Consequences of a Highly Automated Construction Industry," Midwest Economic Policy Institute, January 2018, 7.

6. "The Industry Capitalism Forgot," *Fortune* 36 (August 1947): 61.

7. "Reinventing Construction: A Route to Higher Productivity," McKinsey & Company, February 27, 2017, https://www.mckinsey.com/industries/capital-projects-and-infrastructure/our-insights/reinventing-construction-through-a-productivity-revolution.

8. Leo Sveikauskas et al., "Productivity Growth in Construction," *Journal of Construction Engineering and Management* 142, no. 10 (October 2016).

9. John Fernandez, *Material Architecture* (London: Routledge), 2006.

10. Ryan Smith, *Prefab Architecture: A Guide to Modular Design and Construction* (Hoboken, NJ: Wiley & Sons, 2010), 79.

11. Steven Allen, "Why Construction Industry Productivity Is Declining," *The Review of Economics and Statistics* 67, no. 4 (November 1985): 661, 669.

12. Mark Erlich, *With Our Hands*.

13. Tocci, interview, February 2019.

14. Carl Wilkinson, "Bot the builder: The robot that will replace bricklayers." *Financial Times*, February 23, 2018; Jonathan Waldman, *SAM: One Robot, A Dozen Engineers, and the Race to Revolutionize the Way We Build* (New York: Avid Reader Press, 2020), 182.

15. Ibid.

16. Thomas Steiger, "Construction Skill and Skill Construction," *Work, Employment and Society*, December 1993, 550.

17. Glenn Sanders, "Construction Demolition Robots," www.tractica.com, April 23, 2019; Andrew Evers, "How Autonomous Robots are Changing Construction," CNBC.com, November 30, 2020; Becky Schultz, "Robotic Automation's Potential to Enhance Productivity, Efficiency and Safety on Construction Sites," ForConstructionPros.com, May 26, 2021.

18. Zachary Phillips, "Built Robotics Releases 1st Fully Autonomous Construction Machinery in US," *Construction Dive*, Feb. 26, 2020; Jenn Goodman, "Jobsite Managers Embrace Robotics," *Construction Dive*, June 6, 2019; Groundbreakers Podcast, ForConstructionPros.com; interviews from ConExpo 2020; "Automation Evolves on the Construction Site," OEMOffHighway.com, April 7, 2020.

19. Hiawatha Bray, "Robotic Hard Hat: Automation Does the Tedious Survey Work at Construction Sites," *Boston Globe*, February 24, 2020; Evan Ackerman, "AI Startup Using Robots and Lidar to Boost Productivity on Construction Sites," *IEEE Spectrum*, January 24, 2018; Zachary Phillips, "Boston Dynamics Showcases Robot Dog's Construction Capabilities," *Construction Dive*, February 19, 2020; Zachary Phillips, "Robot Roundup: 5 Recent Innovations in Construction Tech," *Construction Dive*, July 1, 2020.

20. Joe Bousquin, "Drywall Finishing Robot Saves Time, Prevents Injuries," *Construction Dive*, June 16, 2021; Grace Lemasters, M. Atterbury, Angela Booth-Jones, Amit Bhattacharya, N. Ollila-Glenn, Christy Forrester, and Linda Forst, "Prevalence of Work Related Musculoskeletal Disorders in Active Union Carpenters," *Occupational and Environmental Medicine*, June 1, 1998.

21. Jenn Goodman, "New AI-enabled technology quickly identifies bridge defects." *Construction Dive*, July 24, 2019; Jenn Goodman, "Jobsite Managers Embrace Robotics," *Construction Dive*, June 6, 2019; Zachary Phillips, "University of Michigan Unveils Autonomous Roofing Drone Software," *Construction Dive*, October 16, 2019; "Dob Releases Report on Unmanned Aircraft Systems," New York City Department of Buildings press release, November 24, 2021.

22. "The Next Normal in Construction," McKinsey & Company, June 2020.

23. Carl Wilkinson, "Bot the Builder: The Robot That Will Replace Bricklayers," *Financial Times*, February 23, 2018.

24. Charles Towers-Clark, "Construction Co-Bots Need to Be Smarter, More Adaptive," *Forbes*, January 10, 2020.

25. Zachary Phillips, "ConTech Conversations: SDSU Professor Says Robots 'Not Close' to Replacing Human Workers," *Construction Dive*, June 2, 2021.

26. Joe Beeton, "'Automation is Not Innovation' in Offsite, World of Modular Speakers Say," *Construction Dive*, March 18, 2020.

27. https://wearereplicants.wordpress.com/2011/03/10/french-artist-villemards -vision-of-the-future/.

28. Gouveia, interview, September 2020.

29. Donna Laquidara-Carr and Stephen A. Jones, "Measuring the Impact of BIM on Complex Buildings," Dodge Data & Analytics SmartMarket Report, 2015, 4.

30. McLaughlin, interview, February 2021.

31. Connistraro, interview, January 2019.

32. "2020 Annual Construction Technology Report," JBK Consulting, LLC, 2020, 45.

33. Gouveia, interview, September 2020.

34. McLaughlin, interview, February 2021.

35. Sebastian Obando, "Construction Techies Laud $100M in Infrastructure Act, Push for More," *Construction Dive*, November 17, 2021.

36. Tocci, interview, February 2019.

Chapter 7. Building Under a Roof

1. Walter Gropius, "How Do We Build Decent, Beautiful, and Inexpensive Housing?" *Offset: Buch und Werbekunst*, no. 7 (July 1926): 358–70.

2. "Over 123 years of Modular Construction," elements-europe.com.

3. Gilbert Herbert, *The Dream of the Factory-Made House* (Cambridge, MA: MIT Press, 1984), 219.

4. Don Raney and Suzanne Stephens, "Operation Breakthrough: Operation P/R." *Progressive Architecture* 51, April 1, 1970.

5. Mathew Aitchinson, et al., *Prefab Housing and the Future of Building: Product to Process* (London: Lund Humphries, 2018), 93, 121.

6. Gilbert Herbert, *The Dream of the Factory-Made House,* 286–307.

7. Joseph Mason, *History of Housing in the U.S. 1930–1980,* (Houston: Gulf Publishing, 1982), 102, 106.

8. Raney and Stephens, "Operation Breakthrough."

9. "The Buzzword was Factory-Built; Looking Back in Professional Builder's Anniversary Year at Operation Breakthrough and the Fascination with Factory Building," *Professional Builder* 51, August 1986.

10. Comptroller General of the United States, "Operation Breakthrough—Lessons

Learned about Demonstrating New Technology," Department of Housing and Urban Development, Department of Commerce, report to the Congress (Washington, DC: General Accounting Office, 1976).

11. Raney and Stephens, "Operation Breakthrough."

12. Thomas Nutt-Powell, *Manufactured Homes* (Boston: Auburn House Publishing Company, 1982), 43, 45, 92.

13. *Prefabrication and Modularization: Increasing Productivity in the Construction Industry* (McGraw-Hill Construction, 2011), 4, 6.

14. Phil Bernstein, "Future of Construction: Your Next Building Won't Be Built—It Will Be Manufactured," May 3, 2018, https://redshift.autodesk.com.

15. Sebastian Obando, "Modular Construction Use Is 'Booming' in Commercial Building," WealthManagement.com, May 15, 2019.

Linda Lutton, "Factory-Built Three Flats Are Chicago's Newest Affordable Housing," WBEZ Chicago, May 27, 2019.

16. Sebastian Obando, "Modular Construction Use Is 'Booming' in Commercial Building."

17. Ryan Smith, "Permanent Modular Construction," Modular Building Institute, 2015, 2.

18. Joe Bousquin, "Warren Buffett Targets Commercial Modular Construction," *Construction Dive*, June 9, 2021.

19. Zachary Phillips, "Former Tesla Director Joins Modular Developer iBUILT," *Construction Dive*, Jan. 13, 2021.

20. Nick Bertram, Steffen Fuchs, Jan Mischke, Robert Palter, Gernot Strube, and Jonathan Woetzel, "Modular Construction: From Projects to Products," McKinsey & Company, June 18, 2019.

21. https://www.dannyforster.com/.

22. Konrad Putzier, "A Supertall Modular Hotel Is Going Up in Manhattan, if the Rooms Ever Leave Brooklyn," *Wall Street Journal*, June 8, 2021.

23. Charles Bagli, "At Atlantic Yards, Ready to Test Plans for Prefab Tower," *New York Times*, November 27, 2012.

24. Norman Oder, Atlantic Yards/Pacific Park Report, https://atlanticyardsreport .blogspot.com/2020/06/forest-city-skanska-end-bitter-lawsuits.html.

25. Joe Beeton, "Katerra Buys Contractors UEB Builders and Fortune-Johnson," *Construction Dive*, Sept. 6, 2019.

26. Konrad Putzier and Eliot Brown, "How a SoftBank-Backed Construction Startup Burned Through $3 Billion," *Wall Street Journal*, June 29, 2021; Cory Weinberg, "How Katerra's Facade Crumbled," *The Information*, March 4, 2021.

27. Putzier and Brown, June 29, 2021; Sebastian Obando, "What Does Katerra's Demise Mean for the Contech and Modular Industries?" *Construction Dive*, October 13, 2021; "NJ Labor Department Issues Stop-Work Order for Wage Violations, Misclassification of Workers," New Jersey Department of Labor & Workforce Development, February 10, 2020, https://www.nj.gov/labor/lwdhome/press/2020/20200210_stop workorder.shtml.

28. Sebastian Obando, "Modular Builder CEO: 'Katerra's Failure was Spectacular,'" *Construction Dive*, Nov 24, 2021; Sebastian Obando, "UK Modular Builder Expands to US, Hires Former Katerra Staff," *Construction Dive*, November 11, 2021; Nick Bertram, Steffen Fuchs, Jan Mischke, Robert Palter, Gernot Strube, and Jonathan Woetzel, *Modular Construction: From Projects to Products*, McKinsey & Company, June 18, 2019, 11, 5, 28.

29. Sebastian Obando, "Why Modular has not Clicked in Commercial Construction," *Construction Dive*, March 23, 2022.

30. Benson, interview, October 2019.

31. Pace, interview, February 2020; Bradshaw, interview, February 2020; Conor Dougherty, "Piece by Piece, a Factory-Made Answer for a Housing Squeeze," *New York Times*, June 7, 2018.

32. Pace, interview, February 2020; Carroll, interview, September 2020.

33. Matt Gough, at the Advancing Prefabrication Conference, June 15–17, 2021.

34. Amy Marks, at the Advancing Prefabrication Conference, June 15–17, 2021.

35. Grossman, interview, January 2019.

36. Cannistraro, interview, January 2019.

37. Grossman, interview, January 2019.

Chapter 8. Many Rivers to Cross: Organizing and Diversity

1. George Meany, interview, *U.S. News & World Report*, February 21, 1972, 27.

2. Jefferson Cowie, *Stayin' Alive* (New York: The New Press, 2010), 161.

3. Robert McFadden and Peter Brennan, "Union Head and Nixon's Labor Chief," *New York Times*, October 4, 1996.

4. Jeffrey Grabelsky, "Lighting the Spark: COMET Program Mobilizes the Ranks for Construction Organizing," January 1, 1995, https://ecommons.cornell.edu/handle/1813/75815.

5. Jeff Grabelsky, Adam Pagnucco, and Steve Rockafellow, "Fanning the Flames (After Lighting the Spark): Multi-Trade COMET Programs," July 14, 1998, https://ecommons.cornell.edu/handle/1813/75564.

6. John J. Rosen, "'Work for Me Also Means Work for the Community I Come From': Black Contractors, Black Capitalism, and Affirmative Action in the Bay Area," in David Goldberg and Trevor Griffey (eds.), *Black Power at Work: Community Control, Affirmative Action, and the Construction Industry* (Ithaca: Cornell University Press, 2010), 71.

7. Erik Gellman, "The Stone Wall Behind," in Trevor Griffey and David Goldberg (eds.), *Black Power at Work: Community Control, Affirmative Action, and the Construction Industry* (Ithaca: Cornell University Press, 2010), 129.

8. Jeff Grabelsky, review of "Black Power at Work: Community Control, Affirmative Action and the Construction Industry," in *British Journal of Industrial Relations* 50, no. 2, June 2012.

9. Alex Poinsett, "Blacks Battle Blatant Racism in High-Paying Building Jobs," *Ebony* 25, no. 2 (1969): 40.

10. U.S. Commission on Civil Rights, Massachusetts Advisory Committee, *Contract Compliance and Equal Employment Opportunity in the Construction Industry* (Washington, DC, Government Printing Office, 1969), 433.

11. Mark Erlich, *With Our Hands*, 213–14.

12. Mark Erlich, *Labor at the Ballot Box*, 119.

13. Lawrence Mishel, "Racial Underrepresentation in Construction: How Do the Union and Nonunion Sectors Compare?" Economic Policy Institute, Working Economics Blog, October 30, 2013.

14. Joe Bousquin, "Mortenson Shuts Down Meta Jobsite for Second Time Due to Racist Graffiti," *Construction Dive*, November 18, 2021; Joe Bousquin, "Worker Fired from Meta Project for Leaving a Noose on Site," *Construction Dive*, March 22, 2022.

15. Christine Dempsey and Jessika Harkay, "Amazon Construction Site Shut Down Again Wednesday after Eighth Noose was Found," *Hartford Courant*, May 26, 2021.

16. Joe Bousquin, "Noose Found at Another Meta Construction Site," *Construction Dive*, July 1, 2022; Sebastian Obando, "BNBuilders Fires 3 Workers Connected to Noose Incident at Meta Site," *Construction Dive*, July 27, 2022; Joe Bousquin, "$200K Reward Leads to Worker's Termination for Noose at Federal Project," *Construction Dive*, July 20, 2022.

17. See Eduardo Porter, "Can Progress on Diversity Be Union-Made?" *New York Times*, November 6, 2021.

18. Nikki Luke, Carol Zabin, Dalia Velasco, and Robert Collier, "Diversity in California's Clean Energy Workforce: Access to Jobs for Disadvantaged Workers in Renewable Energy Construction," University of California, Berkeley Center for Labor Research and Education, August 2017, 3.

19. Lawrence Mishel, "Diversity in the New York City Union and Nonunion Construction Sectors," Economic Policy Institute report, March 2, 2017.

20. Jeff Grabelsky, review of "Black Power at Work: Community Control, Affirmative Action and the Construction Industry," in *British Journal of Industrial Relations* 50, no. 2, June 2012.

21. Haber and Levinson, *Labor Relations and Productivity in the Building Trades*, 3.

22. Applebaum, *Royal Blue*, 130.

23. Susan Eisenberg, "Pioneering, for the Tradeswomen of '78," *Coffee Break Secrets* (Jamaica Plain, MA: Word of Mouth Productions, 1988), 32–33.

24. Gunseli Berik and Cihan Bilginsoy, "Do Unions Help or Hinder Women in Training? Apprenticeship Programs in the United States," *Industrial Relations* 39, no. 4 (October 2000): 621–22.

25. US Department of Labor, Occupational Safety and Health Administration, https://www.osha.gov/women-in-construction.

26. Institute for Women's Policy Research Fact Sheet, March 2019.

27. Janice Fine, *Worker Centers: Organizing Communities at the Edge of the Dream* (Ithaca: ILR Press, 2006), 3.

28. Natalie Kitroeff, "Immigrants Flooded California Construction. Worker Pay Sank. Here's Why," *Los Angeles Times*, April 22, 2017.

29. Ken Rigmaiden, Keystone Convening on Construction, May 14, 2021.

Chapter 9. Regulators and the Challenge of Enforcement

1. Janice Fine and Jennifer Gordon, "Strengthening Labor Standards through Partnerships with Workers' Organizations," *Politics and Society* 38, no. 4 (2010): 552–85.

2. David Weil and Amanda Pyles, "Why Complain?"

3. Maria Sacchetti, "Governor Moves to Halt Labor Scofflaws: Initiative Targets Employers Who Fail to Pay Taxes," *Boston Globe*, March 13, 2008, http://archive.boston .com/jobs/news/articles/2008/03/13/governor_moves_to_halt_labor_scofflaws/.

4. National Employment Law Project, "Public Task Forces Take on Employee Misclassification: Best Practices," *Policy Brief*, August 2020, https://www.nelp.org/ publication/ public-task-forces-take-on-employee-misclassification-best-practices/.

5. Julie Su, "Enforcing Labor Laws," David Feller Memorial Lecture, Berkeley, CA, April 14, 2015.

6. Janice Fine, "New Approaches to Enforcing Labor Standards: How Co-enforcement Partnerships between Government and Civil Society are Showing the Way Forward," *University of Chicago Legal Forum* 2017 (Article 7): 143–76.

7. Julie Strupp, "The Dotted Line: What to Know about New York's New Construction Wage Theft Law," *Construction Dive*, February 22, 2022.

8. California Department of Industrial Relations, "Labor Commissioner's Office Issues Wage Theft Citations for Subcontractor's Failure to Pay 62 Construction Workers," news release no. 2019-43, May 29, 2019.

9. https://www.nahb.org/advocacy/top-priorities/workforce-development/ Immigration-Reform-is-Key-to-Building-a-Skilled-Workforce.

10. Celine McNicholas, Zane Mokhiber, and Adam Chalkof, "Two Billion Dollars in Stolen Wages were Recovered for Workers in 2015 and 2016—And That's Just a Drop in the Bucket," Economic Policy Institute report, December 13, 2017, https:// www.epi.org/publication/two-billion-dollars-in-stolen-wages-were-recovered-for -workers-in-2015-and-2016-and-thats-just-a-drop-in-the-bucket/; Mark Erlich and Terri Gerstein, "Confronting Misclassification and Payroll Fraud: A Survey of State Labor Standards Enforcement Agencies," Harvard Law School Labor and Worklife Program, 2019.

11. Terri Gerstein, "How District Attorneys and State Attorneys General are Fighting Workplace Abuses," Economic Policy Institute report, May 17, 2021.

12. David Weil and Amanda Pyles, "Why Complain?"

13. U.S. Department of Labor, Wage and Hour Division, Administrator's Interpretation, no. 2015-1, July 15, 2015.

14. Celine McNicholas, Zane Mokhiber, and Adam Chalkof, "Two Billion Dollars in Stolen Wages were Recovered."

15. "US Secretary of Labor withdraws joint employment, independent contractor informal guidance," U.S. Department of Labor, June 7, 2017.

16. National Labor Relations Board, Office of the General Counsel, Advice Memorandum, April 16, 2019.

17. "U.S. Department of Labor issues new wage and hour opinion letter, concludes service providers for a virtual marketplace company are independent contractors," U.S. Department of Labor, April 29, 2019.

18. Velox Express, 368 NLRB No. 61, August 29, 2019.

19. Mark Erlich and Terri Gerstein, "Confronting Misclassification and Payroll Fraud."

20. "Governor Evers signs executive order creating Joint Task Force on Payroll Fraud and Worker Misclassification." Wisconsin Department of Workforce Development, April 15, 2019, https://dwd.wisconsin.gov/news/2019/190415_joint_task force_creation.htm; Montana.gov, "On Tax Day, Governor Bullock Creates Task Force to Ensure Montanans Receive Fair Pay," April 15, 2019, https://news.mt.gov/on-tax-day-governor-bullockcreates-task-force-to-ensure-montanans-receive-fair-pay.

21. Beth LeBlanc, "Nessel Creates Enforcement Unit to Crack Down on Payroll Fraud," *Detroit News*, April 22, 2019, https://www.detroitnews.com/story/news/politics/2019/04/22/nessel-creates-unit-crack-down-payroll-fraud/3541002002/.

22. Nikita Biryukov, "Federal Labor Opinion Won't Affect State Labor Laws," *New Jersey Globe*, May 1, 2019, https://newjerseyglobe.com/governor/federal-labor-opinion-wontaffect-state-labor-laws/.

23. Matthew Haag and Patrick McGeehan, "Uber Fined $649 Million for Saying Drivers Aren't Employees," *New York Times*, November 14, 2019, https://www.nytimes.com/2019/11/14/nyregion/uber-new-jersey-drivers.html.

24. Shayna Jacobs, "Construction Middlemen Put Workers in Danger by Cheating Workers Comp Insurance Providers: DA," *New York Daily News*, September 5, 2019, https://www.nydailynews.com/new-york/ny-labor-broker-worker-comp-charge-20190906-553aosawevbxzo53owd3cpumby-story.html.

25. "D.A. Bragg Announces Indictment in $20M Off-the-Books Compensation Scheme," Manhattan District Attorney's Office, February 16, 2022.

26. Riham Feshir, "Hennepin County's First Labor-Trafficking Case Ends in Guilty Plea," *MPR News*, November 18, 2019, https://www.mprnews.org/story/2019/11/18/contractorricardo-batres-pleads-guilty-in-rare-labor-trafficking-case; Grand Jury Indictment, November 21, 2019, https://wcc-public-news-storage-4081.s3-us-west-2.

27. Katie Johnston and Adam Vaccaro, "State Sues Uber and Lyft, Saying They Cheat Drivers by Calling Them Contractors," *Boston Globe*, July 14, 2020, https://www.bostonglobe.com/2020/07/14/business/state-sues-uber-lyft-over-driver-misclassification-independent-contractors/.

28. Office of the Attorney General of the District of Columbia, "AG Racine An-

nounces National Electrical Contractor Will Pay $2.75 Million to Workers and the District to Resolve Wage Theft Lawsuit," January 15, 2020, https://oag.dc.gov/release/ ag-racine-announces-national-electrical-contractor.

29. Office of the Attorney General of the District of Columbia, "AG Racine Announces Construction Company Must Pay Over $1 Million to Resolve Workers' Rights Lawsuit, Including to Impacted Workers," April 6, 2020, https://oag.dc.gov/ release/ag-racine-announces-construction-company-must-pay.

30. "Changing How Japan Works," *The Economist*, September 29, 2007, 70; Carolyn Said, "Nonprofit Offers Free Course on How to Do Gig Work," *San Francisco Chronicle*, November 22, 2017.

31. Gene Marks, "Tensions Mount as Employers Await a Court Decision on Biden's Vaccine Mandates," *Philadelphia Inquirer*, December 22, 2021.

32. https://joebiden.com/empowerworkers/#.

33. "US Department of Labor to Withdraw Independent Contractor Rule"; "US Department of Labor Announces Final Rule to Rescind March 2020 Joint Employer Rule."

34. Alex Press, "NLRB Says Trucking Companies Are Illegally Misclassifying Port Drivers to Stop Unionization," *Jacobin*, March 28, 2022.

35. "DOL Withdrawal of Trump-Era Independent Contractor Final Rule Unlawful, Court Rules," *National Law Review* XII, no. 91 (April 1, 2022); Caitlin Oprysko, "How IFA Brought Down Biden's Labor Nominee," *Politico*, March 31, 2022; Arthur Delaney and Dave Jamieson, "Senators Joe Manchin, Kyrsten Sinema and Mark Kelly Tank Pro-Worker Labor Nominee," *HuffPost*, March 31, 2022.

36. Leeming, interview, July 2018.

37. "Hearing on Misclassification of Employees: Examining the Costs to Workers, Businesses, and the Economy: Before the Workforce Protections Subcommittee, House Education and Labor Committee, 116th Congress," statement of Matt Townsend, President of the Signatory Wall and Ceiling Contractors Alliance, 2019, 1, https://edlabor.house.gov/imo/media/doc/TownsendTestimony092619.pdf.

38. Patricia Smith, "Testimony to the New Jersey Misclassification Task Force Public Forum," December 5, 2018, National Employment Law Project.

Chapter 10. Restoring a Pathway to the Middle Class

1. Robert Zieger, "George Meany: Labor's Organization Man," in Melvyn Dubofsky and Warren Van Tine (eds.), *Labor Leaders in America* (Urbana: University of Illinois Press, 1987), 326.

2. Gabriel Pleites and Peter Philips, "And All the Plenty Shall Be Forgotten: 80 Fat and 50 Lean Years of Construction Union Wages" [unpublished paper], 2022.

3. North America's Building Trades Unions, *The Campaign Guide: Organizing and Contract Enforcement in the Construction Industry*, 2014, 18.

4. Jessica Beebe, "Non-Union Workers, Rise Up," *Union Built Matters*, www.unionbuiltmatters.org.

5. "Construction Coalition Opposes Biden Administration Project Labor Agreement Schemes," ABC press release, February 16, 2022, https://www.abc.org/News-Media/News-Releases/entryid/19250/construction-coalition-opposes-biden-administration-project-labor-agreement-schemes.

6. Emily Timm, Keystone Convening on Construction, May 13–14, 2021.

7. Manuel Pastor, Ashley Thomas, and Peter Dreier, "LAANE Brain: Understanding the Model and Future of the Los Angeles Alliance for a New Economy," in David Reynolds and Louise Simmons (eds.), *Igniting Justice and Progressive Power* (London: Routledge, 2021), 77.

8. Roxana Tynan, Keystone Convening on Construction, May 13–14, 2021.

9. www.cpwr.com/training/training-overview/.

10. Elird Haxhiu and Peter Philips, "The Role of Collective Bargaining, Remuneration Strategies and Regulations in Fostering Apprenticeship Training in US Construction," unpublished manuscript.

11. Dale Belman, "Registered Apprenticeship in Construction: Built to Last?" www.iceres.org.

12. Leah Rambo, Keystone Convening on Construction, May 13–14, 2021.

13. US Department of Labor, "Employee Benefits Security Administration, Private Pension Plan Bulletin," January 2021.

14. National Electrical Benefit Fund and National Electrical Annuity Plan, "Economic Impacts of Real Estate Investments," June 2021.

Chapter 11. Building a High Road Future

1. Dan Barry and Karen Zraick, "The Men Lost to 20 Bruckner Boulevard," *New York Times*, May 30, 2022.

2. Emily Timm, Keystone Convening on Construction, May 13–14, 2021.

Index

Bradshaw, Jay, 66
Bragg, Alvin, 88
Brennan, Peter, 72–73
Bricklayers Union, 14, 48
bridge work projects, 50
Brown, Charles, 41
Bruno, Angelo, 5
Buffett, Warren, 62
Building & Construction Trades Department (BCTD, AFL-CIO), 74–75
Building Information Modeling (BIM), 52–55, 60, 67, 68, 104
Built Robotics, 48
Bullock, Steve, 88
Burck, Gilbert, 41
Bureau of Labor Statistics (BLS), 12, 47
business cycles, in construction, 12–13, 46, 59, 62–63, 96, 111–12
Business Roundtable, 18–22; anti-union/deregulatory political agenda and, 20–22, 41–43; assumes current name (1972), 18; fragmentation of construction industry and, 18–19; misclassification of workers and (see misclassification of workers); shift to construction manager model and, 19–20, 27–29, 41–42

California: ABC test for independent contractors and, 90; joint employment/co-enforcement in construction and, 85; Los Angeles Alliance for a New Economy (LAANE), 103–4; Proposition 22, 90; Staples Center project (Los Angeles), 104; state-level wage administration programs, 85
Campbell, Karla, 36
Campisano, Nick, 61
Cannistraro, John, 53, 68–69
Cannon Constructors, 66–67
Cantu, David, 36
Canvas, 49
Capece, Matt, 39
Carasquillo, Kelvyn, 5
Carpenters Union (United Brotherhood of Carpenters and Joiners of America): founding (1881), 112; "Big Bill" Hutcheson as president, 71, 73; modular construction and, 66–67; Operation Breakthrough housing program and, 59; regional councils, 3, 38, 66, 95, 98; underground economy and, 86
Carroll, Franklin, 67
Carter administration, 78

cash-only compensation, 7, 35, 37, 39, 40, 42, 43, 51, 65, 79, 84, 88, 91–92, 110
CBAs (Community Benefits/Workforce Agreements), 101–4, 110
Celotex Corporation, 58
Census of Construction Industries, 27
Center for Migration Studies, 34
change orders, 39
Civil Rights Movement, 72, 76–77
Climate Jobs National Resource Center (CJNRC), 111
closed shops (union workers/contractors): competitive disadvantage in requirement to treat workers as employees, 26, 30, 41–42, 91–93, 97; decline in union density, 6, 22, 42–43, 74–75, 95, 97, 112; increase in union density, 6, 15, 47; modular construction and, 66–67; Operation Breakthrough housing program and, 58–59; regional concentrations of, 42; as subject to union collective bargaining agreements, 26; union training programs for CAD and BIM technologies, 54–55. See also construction/building trades unions
Colon, Ruben, 98
Colson, Charles, 72–73
COMET (Construction Organizing Membership Education Training) for unions, 74–75, 96
Community Benefits (or Workforce) Agreements, 101–4, 110
community-labor alliances, 103–4, 110
compensation: Business Roundtable role in, 18–22, 41–43; cash/under-the-table form of, 7, 35, 37, 39, 40, 42, 43, 51, 65, 79, 84, 88, 91–92, 110; Davis-Bacon Act (1931)/mini-Davis-Bacon laws for public construction, 20–21, 103; decline in construction industry (1972–1996) and, 22, 42, 74, 97; deskilling trend in modular construction and, 67–69; earned sick pay, 26, 89; of employees vs. independent contractors, 28 (see also employment benefits); minimum wage, 28, 73; misclassification of workers in (see misclassification of workers); overtime pay, 7, 28, 34–38, 67, 86, 89, 92; payroll fraud and, 37, 39–43, 83–86, 88, 89–92, 100; real wage declines for all workers, 109; real wage growth for union members, 4, 6; relative regional union strength and, 6, 41–43; specialization trend and, 14, 67, 68, 104, 109, 110–11;

state/federal prevailing wage laws, 3, 6, 7, 20–22, 76–77, 83, 99, 101, 103; state regulation of joint employment in construction, 85–86; submarket-level wages, 34, 36–38; underground economy and (*see* underground economy); of undocumented workers, 8, 34, 36–38; unemployment compensation benefits, 26, 28–30, 40, 84, 86, 88, 92; of union vs non-union construction workers, 5–6, 7, 77; upward mobility and, 4–6, 42–43, 96, 106, 109; wage theft and, 6, 7, 34, 37, 85–86, 88–89, 99, 102, 109; worker need for public safety net programs and, 6, 26, 34; workers' compensation benefits, 6, 26, 28–29, 37, 40–41, 83, 88, 92, 102

Computer Aided Design (CAD), 52–55, 60, 66, 68, 104

Computer Numerical Control (CNC) processes, 60–61, 104

Congress of Industrial Organizations (CIO), 71–72

Consigli Construction Company, 89

construction/building trades unions: "American Plan" (1920s), 17; apprenticeship programs (*see* apprenticeship programs); bottom-up vs. top-down organization of, 98–102, 110; as brotherhood/sisterhood, 111–12; COMET (Construction Organizing Membership Education Training) for unions, 74–75, 96; community-labor alliances and, 103–4, 110; conflicts between unions, 96; conservatism of, 72–74; construction industry labor market regulation and, 14–15, 17–18; corruption and, 74; employment benefits to workers (*see* employment benefits); guidelines for organizing (*see* union organizing guidelines); job safety and (*see* safety issues); limits on union membership, 73, 74, 96–97, 103; "low responsible bidder" projects, 83, 102, 110; mergers of, 95–96; number in the US, 96; organizing in (*see* union organizing guidelines); political effectiveness of, 103; protests and strikes, 17–18, 72, 75–77; real wage growth, 4–6; regional union vs. contractor strength in, 6, 28–29; union density trends, 6, 15, 22, 42–43, 47, 74–75, 95, 97, 103–4, 109–10, 112; union workers as "labor aristocrats," 3–4, 42–43, 109

construction industry: business cycles and, 12–13, 46, 59, 62–63, 96, 111–12; Business

Roundtable and, 18–22, 41–43; categories of participants in, 14, 17; change resistance and, 47–48, 53, 54; closed-shop sector (*see* closed shops); college education trend and, 42–43; comparisons with other sectors, 19–20, 45–47, 51, 97; compensation in (*see* compensation); COVID-19 pandemic and, 39–40, 63, 65, 90; decentralized nature of, 13–14, 18–19, 51, 95–96; deskilling trend, 67–69, 110–11; economic impact of, 12–14; employment benefits in (*see* employment benefits); franchisees in, 19–20, 86, 91; future demands for construction workers, 46; gender in (*see* gender diversity in construction); general contractor/construction manager model in, 19–20, 27–29, 35, 41 (*see also* subcontractors); general contractor-subcontractor-journeyman-apprentice system in, 15, 18–19; herd mentality in, 109–10; history of unions in, 3–4 (*see also* construction/building trades unions); hybrid model of employment (core and periphery workers), 25, 27, 91, 98; labor productivity trends, 46–47, 50–51 (*see also* technology in construction); lack of reliable data on, 27, 40–42, 47; open-shop sector (*see* open shops); in the post-World War II Great Compression, 4, 11–12; race and ethnicity in (*see* racial/ethnic diversity in construction); safety issues in (*see* safety issues), seasonality of, 12–13, 47–48; skilled worker shortage, 42–43; small businesses in, 13–15, 27, 48, 51, 53, 75, 91, 99; structural innovations in buildings, 11–12; subsectors of, 13; technology and (*see* technology in construction); undocumented workers in (*see* undocumented construction workers); unemployment rates in, 12–13; union density of, 6, 15, 22, 41–43, 74–75, 95, 97, 103–4, 109–10, 112; unions in (*see* construction/building trades unions; union organizing guidelines); visibility to the public, 5

construction manager model, 27–29, 35; Business Roundtable and, 19–20, 27–29, 41–42; franchisees in, 19–20, 86, 91; labor brokers in (*see* labor brokers); nature of the construction manager, 19–20. *See also* independent contractors in building trades

Construction Robotics, 48

Cort, John, 76
COVID-19 pandemic, 39–40, 63, 65, 90
coyote system, 34

Daiwa House Industry (Japan), 58
Davis-Bacon Act (1931), 20–21, 103
Department of Labor (DOL). *See* U.S. Department of Labor
Dillard, Hub, 4
District of Columbia: joint employment/co-enforcement in construction and, 85; legal action for wage theft and misclassification, 88–89
Doxel, 49
drones, 50, 54
drywall/Sheetrock workers, 28–30, 34–35, 36, 38–39, 49, 67, 89
Dynamic Contracting, 89

Economic Policy Institute, 87
Eisenberg, Susan, 78–79
electricians/electrical subcontractors, 53; gender diversity and, 78–79; legal action for wage theft and misclassification, 88–89; Operation Breakthrough housing program and, 59
Emanuello, Joseph, 48
employment benefits: anti-discrimination protection, 28; dispute resolution, 15; health insurance, 6, 15, 26, 28, 106; pension and annuity benefits, 6, 15, 28, 105–6, 110; relative regional union strength and, 6, 41–43; right to form a union, 28; Social Security/Medicare tax payments, 26; training (*see* training programs). *See also* compensation
ethnicity. *See* racial/ethnic diversity in construction
E-Verify system, 37
Evers, Tony, 88
excavation equipment, 11, 49, 50
exoskeletons, 50

FactoryOS, 66–67
Fair Labor Standards Act (1938), 27, 29, 84, 87
FedEx headquarters project (Memphis), 36
Fernandez, John, 47
First Construction, 38–39
Fiscal Policy Institute, 37
Fissured Workplace, The (Weil), 86–87
Fletcher, Arthur, 76
Flextronics, 64
Florida, legal actions for fraud in construction, 38–39, 89

Floyd, George, 77
Forest City, 63–64
Forster, Danny, 63
franchisees, 19–20, 86, 91
Freedman, Audrey, 25
French-Canadian construction workers, 29–30, 37–38
Future of Work Task Force (MIT), 46

gender diversity in construction: construction industry opposition to, 47–48; gender discrimination in construction and, 4–7, 78–79; lack of, in the post–World War II Great Compression, 4; pre-apprenticeship programs and, 78, 79, 105
general contractor-subcontractor-journeyman-apprentice system: bidding practices, 18–19, 89, 92–93, 100–101; change order impact on subcontractors, 39; construction manager model vs., 19–20, 27–29, 35, 41; decline in general contractor share of construction worker employment, 19; joint employment/co-enforcement in construction and, 34, 85–86, 90–91; multi-tier subcontracting and, 19, 25, 34, 39, 85; using union firms, 101. *See also* independent contractors in building trades
General Panel, 58
Georgine, Robert, 74, 75
gig economy: conceptions of independent contracting and, 89–90; misclassification of workers and, 30, 83, 87, 88, 90–91; rideshare firms in, 30, 87–88, 90
Gilbane Building Company, 89
Gomez, Frank, 7, 34–35
Gonzalez, Gonzalo, 62
Gott, Edwin, 18
Gouveia, Jeff, 52, 54
Government Accountability Office, 21
Grabelsky, Jeff, 74
Gray, Darryl, 8–9
Great Depression, 6, 12–13, 57, 71, 76, 101
Great Recession (2007–2009), 12–13, 79
green construction/clean energy projects, 104, 110, 111
Greenland USA, 64
Gropius, Walter, 57, 60
Grossman, Jim, 68, 69
guest worker programs, 79

Haber, William, 41–42
Hadall, Jeremy, 50
Hard Rock Hotel collapse of 2020 (New Orleans), 7–9

layoffs, 7, 28, 65
Leeming, Simon, 29–30, 37–38, 92
Lekfus, John, 51
Levinson, Harold, 41–42
Lewis, John L., 71
limited liability companies (LLCs), 28–29, 35
Lindsay, John, 72, 73
local business agents, 73–74
Lockheed Aircraft, 58
Los Angeles Alliance for a New Economy (LAANE), 103–4
Louisiana: Hard Rock Hotel collapse of 2020 (New Orleans), 7–9; Hurricane Katrina labor brokers and, 37; jury indictment for misclassification of workers, 88
Lyft, 88, 90

Manchin, Joe, 91
Manufacturing Technology Centre (UK), 50–51
Marek (Houston), 25–26
Marek, Stan, 25–26
Marks, Amy, 68
Marks, Michael, 64–65
Marriott hotel modular project (New York City), 63
Massachusetts: Boston Jobs Coalition, 76; consultants to contractors and, 29–30, 37–38, 92; Division of Unemployment Assistance (DUA), 40; Future of Work Task Force (MIT), 46; Massachusetts Building Trades Council, 3; Massachusetts Misclassification Law (2004), 84, 88; prevailing wage law, 3, 76–77, 83; Responsible Employer Ordinance (Cambridge), 83; state-level construction safety enforcement, 84–85, 86; Task Force on the Underground Economy, 84
master-journeyman-apprentice system, 15
McGovern, George, 73
McGraw-Hill Construction, 60
McGuire, Peter, 112
McKinsey & Company: construction industry productivity and, 46–47, 50–51; McKinsey Global Institute, 46–47; modular construction and, 63, 65
McLaughlin, John, 53, 54, 68
Meany, George, 71–74, 96
Medicare taxes, 26
Meta (formerly Facebook), 77
Michigan: Payroll Fraud Enforcement Unit, 88; University of Michigan roofing drones, 50

Midwest Economic Policy Institute, 46
Migration Policy Institute, 34
Miller, Steve, 21
minimum wage, 28, 73
Minnesota: George Floyd murder, 77; legal theory of human trafficking for immigrant construction workers, 88
misclassification of workers, 33–43; complaint-based model of, 84, 86–87; consultants to contractors and, 29–30, 37–38, 90, 92; costs to the economy, 39, 40–41, 83, 84, 86–87; COVID-19 pandemic and, 39–40; as employment strategy, 25–30, 40; federal-state cooperation in reforming, 86–87; federal vs. state guidelines for, 87–88; gig economy and, 30, 83, 87–88, 90–91; and the Immigration Reform and Control Act (IRCA), 33–34, 36–37; IRS reclassification penalties and, 21–22; joint employment/co-enforcement and, 85–86, 90–91; legal actions for, 84, 88–89; of licensed construction trade workers, 88–89; limited liability companies (LLCs) and, 28–29, 35; nature of, 21; Revenue Act of 1978, Section 530 and, 21–22, 25, 26, 84; rideshare workers in the gig economy, 30, 87–88, 90; "safe harbor" protections for employers and, 21, 29–30, 84; state-level task forces and, 85–88; by tech companies, 90; truck drivers and, 90–91; U.S. Department t of Labor consent judgments for, 28–29. See also independent contractors in building trades
MiTek, 62
MIT Future of Work Task Force, 46
MIT Technology Review, 46
mobile homes, 58, 59–60
Modular Building Institute (MBI), 61–62, 66
modular construction, 60–69; challenges of, 62–65; cost savings from, 60–61, 67–68; deskilling of workers and, 67–69; expedited schedules for, 62, 63; financing issues, 62–65; future prospects for, 66–68; "jump factory" on site and, 67–68; panelized walls in, 61, 67, 68; prefabrication and, 58, 67, 68, 110; shift from build-to-order (BTO) to engineer-to-order (ETO), 62; shift from contracting to manufacturing, 68–69; stages of, 61–62; transportation costs, 62, 63
Modulous, 65
Montana, Task Force on Integrity in Wage Reporting and Employee Certification, 88

Montgomery Ward, homebuilding packages, 57–58
Motor Carrier Act (1980), 90–91
Music City Convention Center (Nashville), 35

National Academy of Sciences, 45–46
National Apprenticeship Act (1937), 104
National Association of Home Builders (NAHB), 85
National Carpentry Contractors, 38
National Electrical Benefit Fund, 105
National Employment Law Project (NELP), 85
National Institute of Building Sciences (NIBS), 54
National Labor Relations Board (NLRB), 38, 87–88, 90, 98
National Science Foundation, 51
Nessel, Dana, 88
Nevada, Las Vegas construction boom, 80
New Deal, 71
New Jersey: enforcement of state labor laws, 88; New Jersey Department of Labor, 65; recommendation for interagency cooperation, 92–93
New York City: Atlantic Yards/Pacific Park development (Brooklyn), 63–64; Building and Construction Trades Council, 72; legal actions for workers' compensation fraud, 88; modular Marriott hotel project, 63; New York Building Congress, 37; New York City Department of Buildings drones, 50; New York Plan, 72–73; OSHA investigation of construction-related fatalities, 109; payroll fraud actions, 88
New York State: joint employment in construction and, 85; state-level task force on construction, 84–85, 86
Nixon administration, 18, 72–73
nonresidential construction, 13, 14
North America's Building Trades Unions (NABTU), 77–78, 97, 105

Obama administration, 87
Occupational Safety and Health Administration (OSHA), 9, 102, 104, 109
Oliver (mobile robot), 49
open shops (non-union workers/contractors): anti-union political agenda and, 20–22, 41–43; compensation and (see compensation); competitive advantage in hiring independent contractors, 26, 30, 41–42, 91–93, 97; market share in construction, 41–42; organizing guidelines and (see union organizing guidelines); private construction projects and, 20; safety issues (see safety issues); undocumented workers (see undocumented construction workers). See also subcontractors
Operation Breakthrough housing program, 58–59
Organisation for Economic Co-operation and Development (OECD), 46
overtime pay, 7, 28, 34–38, 67, 86, 89, 92

Pace, Larry, 66–67
Painters Union, 49, 72, 80
Palma, Delmer, 8–9
Pasona, 89
Patrick, Deval, 84
Paul Johnson Drywall, 29
payroll fraud, 37, 39–43, 83–86, 88, 89–92, 100
pension and annuity benefits, 6, 15, 28, 105–6, 110
Pew Research Center, 33–34
Philadelphia Plan, 72, 76
Philips, Peter, 21
Plumbers Union, 59
Power Design, Inc., 88–89
power tools and labor-saving devices, 29, 30, 47–48, 50
prefabrication/factory-built housing, 57–58, 67, 68, 110
prevailing wage laws, 3, 6, 7, 20–22, 76–77, 83, 99, 101, 103
private construction projects, 13; anti-union political agenda and, 20–22, 41–43; open (non-union) shops and, 20; prevailing wage laws and, 21–22
PRO Act, 90
Prodromos, Dean, 21
Professional Builder, 59
Progressive Architecture, 59–60
Project Labor Agreements (PLAs), 101–4, 110
public construction projects, 13; BIM mandated for UK projects, 54; Davis-Bacon Act (1931)/mini–Davis-Bacon laws, 20–21, 103; gender diversity and, 78; prevailing wage laws and, 3, 6, 20–22, 76–77, 83, 99, 101, 103; Project Labor Agreements (PLAs), 101–4, 110; Revenue Act of 1978, Section 530 and, 21–22, 25, 26, 84

racial/ethnic diversity in construction: African American construction workers and,

racial/ethnic diversity in construction (*continued*)
75–78, 80; Civil Rights Movement, 72, 76–77; ethnic affiliations of specific construction trades, 29–30, 37–38; foreign-language speaking union locals and, 4; increasing minority participation in New York City construction trades, 72; lack of, in the post World War II Great Compression, 4; Latino construction workers and (*see* Latino construction workers); New York Plan and, 72–73; Philadelphia Plan and, 72, 76; pre-apprenticeship programs and, 78, 105; protests and, 75–77; racial discrimination and, 4, 6–7, 75; segregated union locals, 4, 75

Racine, Karl, 89
Rad Technology, 51
Rambo, Leah, 78
Ramirez, Gustavo, 36
Ratner, Bruce, 63–64
RCML, 49
Reagan administration, 20
Reppert, R. I., 30
residential construction, 13, 14. *See also* housing construction
responsible bidder programs, 83, 102, 110
retirement benefits, 6, 15, 28, 105–6, 110
Revenue Act of 1978, Section 530, 21–22, 25, 26, 84
Rhode Island, compensation laws, 7
rideshare firms, in the gig economy, 30, 87–88, 90
Rigmaiden, Ken, 80
Rise Construction, 68, 69
robotics, 46–51
Romney, George, 58–59
Romney, Mitt, 84
roofers and roofing, 50
Roswell Drywall LLC (Georgia), 35

safety issues: COVID-19 pandemic and, 39–40; deaths of construction workers, 7–8, 9, 35–36, 109; decline in federal policing of workplaces and, 84; "frequent flyers" (problematic contractors) and, 35–36; and the Hard Rock Hotel collapse of 2020 (New Orleans), 7–9; lack of harnesses and safety devices, 35–36; at the La Quinta Hotel (Nashville), 36; National Employment Law Project (NELP), 85; OSHA and, 9, 102, 104, 109; reality of high-risk conditions in construction, 9; regional levels of union strength and, 6;

state-level enforcement and, 84–85, 86; technology and, 48, 49; undocumented workers and, 7–9, 35–36, 38, 39–40; in union vs. non-union sector, 6, 7, 109; workers' compensation for on-the-job injuries (*see* workers' compensation insurance)
"salting" non-union contractors, 99
San Diego State University, 51
Sears Roebuck, homebuilding packages, 57–58
seasonality, 12–13, 67
Section 530, Revenue Act of 1978, 21–22, 25, 26, 84
Semi-Autonomous Mason (SAM), 48
Sepulveda, Sandra, 36
Sheet Metal and Air Conditioning Contractors' National Association (SMACNA), 26
Sheet Metal Workers, 75, 78
sick time, 26, 89
side jobs, 27
Signatory Wall and Ceiling Contractors Alliance, 92
Simonson, Ken, 43
Sinema, Kyrsten, 91
Sizemore, Greg, 43
Skanska, 64
Skender, Mark, 61
Skender Manufacturing, 61, 65
small/family businesses in construction, 13–15, 27, 48, 51, 53, 75, 91, 99
Smith, Adam, 45, 48
Smith, Patricia, 92–93
Social Security taxes, 26
SoftBank, 64–65
specialization trend, 14, 67, 68, 104, 109, 110–11
Spot (robot dog), 49
Staples Center (Los Angeles), 104
Starrett, William, 14
"stripping" foremen and lead workers, 99–100
Su, Julie, 85
subcontractors: for business services, 25; cost pressures on, 39; deskilling trend in modular construction and, 67–69; as former union members, 14, 15; in the general contractor/construction manager model, 19–20, 27–30, 35, 41; and the general contractor-subcontractor-journeyman-apprentice system, 15; multitier, 19, 25, 34, 39, 85. *See also* labor brokers
Suffolk Construction, 52

Sullivan & McLaughlin, 53, 68–69
summer help, 27
Sweden: *Miljonprogrammet* (Million Homes Program), 58

technology in construction, 45–55; 3D imaging and modeling, 49, 50, 52–54; 4D schedule modeling, 54; 5D cost modeling, 54; 6D facility management modeling, 54; artificial intelligence (AI), 46, 50; autonomous vehicles and heavy equipment, 49, 50; Building Information Modeling (BIM), 52–55, 60, 67, 68, 104; challenges of using, 51, 53, 110–11; Computer Aided Design (CAD), 52–55, 60, 66, 68, 104; Computer Numerical Control (CNC) processes, 60–61, 104; drones, 50, 54; excavation equipment, 11, 49, 50; exclusive nature of, 53; independent contracting and misclassification by technology companies, 90; Katerra and, 64–65; for layout and documentation, 49, 50; power tools and labor-saving devices, 29, 30, 47–48, 50; project coordination and, 52–54; projections for impact of, 45–48, 51–55; resistance to change and, 47–48, 53, 54; robotics, 46–51; safety issues and, 48, 49; technological unemployment and, 45–46, 48; training programs for, 54–55, 104; Villemard's conception of, 51–52
Teicholz, Paul, 47
temporary staffing agencies, 89
Tennessee: FedEx headquarters project (Memphis), 36; La Quinta Hotel project (Nashville), 36; Music City Convention Center project (Nashville), 35; Tennessee Bureau of Workers Compensation, 41
Terkel, Studs, 4
Texas: Better Builder Program, 102, 110; Workers Defense Project, 34, 102, 110. *See also* undocumented construction workers
Third World Workers' Association, 76
Tilson, Betsey, 40
Timm, Emily, 110
Tocci, John, 48, 53
Total station (optical instrument), 50
Townsend, Matthew, 92
Tractica, 48
training programs: for CAD and BIM in construction, 54–55, 104; COMET (Construction Organizing Membership Education Training) for unions, 74–75, 96; job training of unions and union employers, 3, 14–15, 36, 45, 53, 54–55,

78–80, 96, 102–3 (*see also* apprenticeship programs; journeyworkers); in non-union environments, 102, 104–5; off-site/modular production and, 110–12; OSHA safety programs, 102, 104; for union staff members, 74–75, 96, 97
Troy, Leo, 6
Trump administration, 87–88, 90–91
Turmail, Brian, 43
Turner, Chuck, 76
Turpin, Mark, 3
Tybot (bar-tying robot), 50
Tynan, Roxana, 104

Uber (ride-sharing), 87, 88, 90
underground economy, 6; black market for fake employment documents, 37; cash/under-the-table compensation, 7, 35, 37, 39, 40, 42, 43, 51, 65, 79, 84, 88, 91–92, 110; growth of immigrant workforce and, 36–37; Massachusetts Task Force on the Underground Economy, 84; payroll fraud and, 37, 39–43, 83–86, 88, 89–92, 100; wage theft and, 6, 7, 34, 37, 85–86, 88–89, 99, 102, 109
undocumented construction workers, 33–39, 42; black market for fake employment documents, 37; compensation of, 8, 34, 36–38 (*see also* compensation); deportation threats, 8–9, 37, 79; E-Verify system and, 37; housing provided for, 36, 38; Immigration Reform and Control Act (IRCA) and, 33–34, 36–37; labor brokers and (*see* labor brokers); misclassification of (*see* misclassification of workers); proportion of national construction workforce, 34; regional concentrations of, 34; safety issues and, 7–9, 35–36, 38, 39–40 (*see also* safety issues); U.S. Border Patrol and, 8–9; working conditions for, 7–9, 34, 35–36. *See also* immigrants/immigration; independent contractors in building trades
unemployment: in the construction industry, 12–13; in the Great Depression, 12–13, 76; technology and job replacement, 45–46, 48; underpayment of unemployment taxes, 26, 29–30, 40, 84, 86, 88, 92; unemployment compensation benefits, 26, 28–30, 40, 84, 86, 88, 92
union organizing guidelines, 95–103; area master agreements and, 98; Better Builder Program (Texas) as union alternative, 102, 110; bottom-up vs. top-down

MARK ERLICH is a Wertheim Fellow at The Center for Labor and a Just Economy at Harvard Law School and the retired Executive Secretary-Treasurer of the New England Regional Council of Carpenters. His books include *Labor at the Ballot Box: The Massachusetts Prevailing Wage Campaign of 1988* and *With Our Hands: The Story of Carpenters in Massachusetts.*

The Working Class in American History

The Labor Question in America: Economic Democracy in the Gilded Age
  Rosanne Currarino
Banded Together: Economic Democratization in the Brass Valley   *Jeremy Brecher*
The Gospel of the Working Class: Labor's Southern Prophets in New
  Deal America   *Erik Gellman and Jarod Roll*
Guest Workers and Resistance to U.S. Corporate Despotism   *Immanuel Ness*
Gleanings of Freedom: Free and Slave Labor along the Mason-Dixon Line,
  1790–1860   *Max Grivno*
Chicago in the Age of Capital: Class, Politics, and Democracy during the Civil
  War and Reconstruction   *John B. Jentz and Richard Schneirov*
Child Care in Black and White: Working Parents and the History of Orphanages
  Jessie B. Ramey
The Haymarket Conspiracy: Transatlantic Anarchist Networks
  Timothy Messer-Kruse
Detroit's Cold War: The Origins of Postwar Conservatism   *Colleen Doody*
A Renegade Union: Interracial Organizing and Labor Radicalism   *Lisa Phillips*
Palomino: Clinton Jencks and Mexican-American Unionism in the
  American Southwest   *James J. Lorence*
Latin American Migrations to the U.S. Heartland: Changing Cultural Landscapes
  in Middle America   *Edited by Linda Allegro and Andrew Grant Wood*
Man of Fire: Selected Writings   *Ernesto Galarza, ed. Armando Ibarra and
  Rodolfo D. Torres*
A Contest of Ideas: Capital, Politics, and Labor   *Nelson Lichtenstein*
Making the World Safe for Workers: Labor, the Left, and Wilsonian
  Internationalism   *Elizabeth McKillen*
The Rise of the Chicago Police Department: Class and Conflict, 1850–1894
  Sam Mitrani
Workers in Hard Times: A Long View of Economic Crises   *Edited by Leon Fink,
  Joseph A. McCartin, and Joan Sangster*
Redeeming Time: Protestantism and Chicago's Eight-Hour Movement, 1866–1912
  William A. Mirola
Struggle for the Soul of the Postwar South: White Evangelical Protestants and
  Operation Dixie   *Elizabeth Fones-Wolf and Ken Fones-Wolf*
Free Labor: The Civil War and the Making of an American Working Class
  Mark A. Lause
Death and Dying in the Working Class, 1865–1920   *Michael K. Rosenow*
Immigrants against the State: Yiddish and Italian Anarchism in America
  Kenyon Zimmer
Fighting for Total Person Unionism: Harold Gibbons, Ernest Calloway,
  and Working-Class Citizenship   *Robert Bussel*
Smokestacks in the Hills: Rural-Industrial Workers in West Virginia
  Louis Martin

The University of Illinois Press
is a founding member of the
Association of University Presses.

───────────────────────────

University of Illinois Press
1325 South Oak Street
Champaign, IL 61820-6903
www.press.uillinois.edu